TEMPERAMENT

Theory and Practice

BRUNNER/MAZEL
BASIC PRINCIPLES INTO PRACTICE SERIES

BRUNNER/MAZEL
BASIC PRINCIPLES INTO PRACTICE SERIES
VOLUME 12

TEMPERAMENT

Theory and Practice

STELLA CHESS, M.D.
AND
ALEXANDER THOMAS, M.D.

BRUNNER/MAZEL, *Publishers* • NEW YORK

Library of Congress Cataloging-in-Publication Data

Chess, Stella.
    Temperament : theory and practice / Stella Chess and Alexander
Thomas.
        p.   cm. — (Brunner/Mazel basic principles into practice
series ; v. 12)
    Includes bibliographical references and indexes.
    ISBN 0-87630-835-3 (pbk.)
    1. Temperament in children—Longitudinal studies. 2. Individual
differences in children—Longitudinal studies. I. Thomas,
Alexander,   . II. Title.   III. Series.
BF1723.T53C48   1996
155.4′182—dc20   96-28525
                                                                CIP

Published by
BRUNNER/MAZEL, INC.
19 Union Square West
New York, New York 10003

Manufactured in the United States of America
        10   9   8   7   6   5   4   3   2   1

CONTENTS

Part I

Basic Concepts of Theory and Practice of Temperament

1

INTRODUCTION

The concept of temperament has by now been widely recognized as one of the basic aspects of the psychological mechanism of behavioral functioning. The temperamental profiles of infants, children, adolescents, and adults show specific individual behavioral characteristics. These formulations have been accepted as a result of the reports of the findings of the systematic study by Chess and Thomas in their long-term investigation, the New York Longitudinal Study, begun in 1956, and pursued to the present decade.

A number of researchers and clinicians had earlier commented on their own observations of the individual behavioral characteristics of children. In the 1930s two pioneer workers in child development, Shirley (1933) and Gesell and Ames (1937) reported specific differences in individual infants. Freud (1937, 1950) asserted that "each individual ego is endowed from the beginning with its own peculiar dispositions and tendencies" (vol. 5, p. 316). Pavlov (1927) postulated the existence of congenitally determined types of nervous system as basic to the course of subsequent behavioral development.

In the 1940s and 1950s a number of studies appeared that reported observations of individual differences in infants and young children in specific, discrete areas of functioning, such as perceptual responses (Bergman & Escalona, 1949), motility (Fries & Woolf, 1953), drive endowment (Alpert, Neubauer, & Wiel, 1956), and mildness and intensity of emotional tone (Meili, 1959). David Levy (1943), the director of one of the earliest mental health clinics for children, reported his pioneering study of boys whose behavior disorders appeared to be related to maternal overprotection. These two major outcomes were due to the children's own behavioral characteristics. The passive boys became "obedient automatons", and the assertive and combatant boys became family tyrants.

These various reports emphasized that individual differences appeared to be present at birth and were influenced, but not determined, by postnatal experience.

In addition, the need for anterospective longitudinal studies in the investigation of the origins and evolution of behavioral disorders in children has been recognized by a number of workers the University of California at Berkeley (McFarlane, Allen, & Honzig, 1962), the Fels Institute (Kagan & Moss, 1962), and the Meninger Clinic (Murphy, 1962). Longitudinal studies at these centers have made a number of contributions to our knowledge of normal and aberrant behavioral development. The possible significance of the temperamental characteristics of the child in interaction with parental functioning has been indicated. However, each of these studies has been militated against either by small sample size or by the absence of systematic psychiatric evaluation of the children, which has not permitted generalization of the findings.

Beyond these specific professional reports, experienced parents, baby nurses, and pediatricians have often observed, in the course of their caretaking activities, that different infants showed even strikingly unique behaviors from the first weeks of birth onward. But no one had recorded this in any serious or systematic study.

As to the professional report of those years, they were too narrow and limited to provide a basis for any systematic and comprehensive understanding of behavioral individuality in early childhood, or the significance of such individuality for psychological development.

2

THE INITIAL CONCEPT OF TEMPERAMENT

In past centuries the explanations for individuality in behavioral development have basically advocated one of two views—nature or nurture. The first theory considered the newborn to be an homunculus, literally an adult in miniature. The opposite view, nurture, held that the newborn was a tabulu rasa, as the 17th century British philosopher John Locke put it—a clean slate on which the environment would inscribe its influence until the adult personality was etched to completion. This debate of nature versus nurture, heredity versus environment, was dominated by the intrinsic hereditary argument until the 19th century. Starting in the 20th century with the extensive studies of Freud, Pavlov, and many students of child development, the concept of nurture began to influence this viewpoint. This approach strengthened and from the 1920s on began to dominate the field of child development.

By the early 1950s the environmentalist view was accepted, with a few exceptions. Any organic contribution to any explanation of a child's function was almost universally considered to be antithetical to psychological development.

This is how we were taught in the 1940s—behavioral differences in children were always due to the environment, usually the mother, although sometimes some spe-

cial extrafamilial event was also implicated. However, as
we went into clinical practice with new patients, the standard concepts, whether psychoanalysis, behaviorism or
learning theory, or attachment theory, just didn't make
sense. Many young mothers tortured themselves with unnecessary guilt and self-reproach because those authorita-
tive experts had proclaimed that one or another of these
theories necessarily blamed the mother for any presumed
abnormality in the child.

One mother, Mrs. T., who came to see me (S.C.) was
a horrendous example, even a caricature, of those who
suffered the uncompromising verdict of "bad mother."
She was in a state of anguish and guilt and believed her
son, Peter, 8 years old, to be in "deep psychological trouble," with his future in jeopardy. She believed this had
to be due to her faulty mothering. She was familiar with
psychoanalytic theory and reported that Peter had a serious problem in expressing anger and hostility. While she
was prepared to deal with the "terrible twos," this early
period had gone by in serenity. He had rarely had a tantrum, and he was a reasonable child as to behavioral limits and doing his assigned chores. When he had an argument, it was with quiet logic and without anger. She had
herself suffered from constant criticism in her boisterous,
contentious tomboy childhood and had been determined
to avoid such repressive maternal behavior. But here was
her quiet, well-behaved son failing to express the normal
stages of wrestling with authority so well described by
Anna Freud. There were no other "symptoms." Peter had
friends with whom he played some active games, but he
preferred reading, learning in school, and long discussions with his father. He had no nightmares, learning
problems, fears, phobias. He was not afraid of new experiences. His father did not consider him a problem and
found few faults with Mrs. T.'s attitudes toward either
Peter or his more rambunctious younger brother.

A play session during which he entered freely into discussion showed a normal 8-year-old with wide-ranging

intellectual interests in keeping with his age and a high intellectual status: Why did dinosaurs come to an end? What was the big bang theory of the universe? Why did his mother always tell him to go out and play when he was busy playing checkers with a friend?

The real problem was to convince Mrs. T. that a normal child comes in a variety of behavioral styles. Peter was quiet in expressiveness, motorically middle of the spectrum, persistent in his expression of interests, and rarely forgot to take out the garbage when it was his turn. He was as normal as the more active and forgetful brother, Dennis, who loved roughhouse play. The importance of convincing Mrs. T. to accept and appreciate Peter's style extended beyond merely providing her with reassurance. She had, in fact, begun to make Peter feel that she disapproved of him. Having interpreted her psychological reading as giving a template of the active, argumentative child as a norm, I realized that, in her campaign to free his presumed repressed aggression, she was really undercutting his confidence in being his own kind of individual.

The discussion had a favorable outcome. The mother, a bit doubtful at first, after several sessions and with her husband's support, did relax and began to enjoy her quiet and stimulating child.

Of course, in some cases, a child's behavioral problem is due to some abnormal maternal handling, or some other pathogenic environmental circumstance. At other times, a child's development pursues a consistently healthy direction, in the face of severe parental disturbance, family disorganization, and social stress. One case was particularly striking. The parents had consulted one of us (A.T.) because of severe marital disharmony. Almost any small disagreement escalated into shouting and denigrating name-calling. Both parents agreed that their two children were often present on those occasions.

I had many therapeutic sessions with each parent separately and also jointly. But all my efforts were completely unsuccessful. Inevitably, a contentious divorce ensued. Despite statements by each parent that the psychological well-being of the children was of primary importance, there were bitter legal battles over child support and visitation. And after the legalities had been settled, fighting involved the children. During the children's visit to the father, he would inquire into the mother's social life; on their return home the mother would criticize the father's laxity as to bedtime, eating arrangements, and prodigality with gifts.

Both parents tried to enlist me as a partisan in the battles over their children's lives. I did my best, as a neutral ally for the welfare of the children. I only succeeded in modestly mitigating the severity of the parents' battles over the children. My deepening concern was over the effect of the severe stress imposed on the children by this parental disturbance and family dysfunction. The parents did agree to refer the children to S.C. for her evaluation, advice, and, if necessary, treatment.

To our surprise, S.C.'s careful clinical evaluation showed that the two children, Gabrielle, age 7, and Greg, age 9, were functioning well in all areas. They each had friends with whom visits were exchanged and school functioning was satisfactory in both the academic and the social spheres. There were no symptoms of either anxiety or aggression, and both were quite outspoken and accurate in their assessment of the family situation. Prior to the divorce, each time their parents started fighting the children had been in the habit of going off to play elsewhere in peace. They reported they enjoyed any time spent separately with each parent. Although they wished their parents would stop fighting, they accepted this as a given—that's the way life went. Since each was outgoing, enjoyed new experiences and new people, adapted quickly to new circumstances, and had a predominantly cheerful demeanor, they easily became involved in pleasant activities with other children and adults. Since friends of theirs also had divorced parents, they shared similar stories. They were quite open about their willingness to take advantage of their father's overindulgence but in fact were relieved to return home to their mother's regular schedule. Our conclusion was that their individual behavioral qualities, which brought so many positive responses from both the larger environment and each parent individually, had given them distance and protection from the unpleasantness of the parental battle. It simply wasn't their problem and they made sure to avoid becoming pawns in the parental wars.

S.C. decided that the children had no need for psychotherapy. Both were coping effectively on their own with this severe parental dysfunction, and she only reassured the children that their attitudes and activities were splendid. At a follow-up 2 years later, the evaluation showed them to be continuing to develop and mature positively, and her prognosis was very favorable.

Finally, we saw many, many instances in which a child's psychopathology occurred even with good parents. For example, there was Carla, 4 years old, brought to my (S.C.) office by her parents, with a rather serious behavioral problem at nursery school and at social occasions. She had been having a hard time each morning when getting ready for school. She refused breakfast, made a fuss about dressing, and cried when her mother left her at school. The teacher reported that Carla spent the day on the fringe of the various activities, with no participation in them and an unhappy look. In addition, Carla demonstrated this similar distressing behavior in many new situations. When invited to a birthday party, she raised objections, became whiny, and hid behind her mother.

With these problems, the mother sought advice and was recommended to a good psychoanalyst. The therapist judged Carla's problem to be separation anxiety due to insecure attachment to the mother. The recommended treatment was for the mother to search into her unconscious reasons for wishing to maintain Carla's dependency on her. After some months of psychoanalytic sessions, no significant insights had been achieved, and the mother was dissatisfied with the therapist's theory and treatment. Then a friend recommended that she consult me and she did.

In my clinical interview, I could find no evidence of any unhealthy psychological attitudes or behavior in the mother. She had done all the sensible things to encourage Carla's growing independence and maturity, and there was no evidence of any attitudes or behavior to tie Carla with undesirable dependency to her. Beyond that, the detailed descriptions of Carla's behavior difficulties revealed clearly that her disturbances always occurred with new situations. Whenever she visited familiar friends and/or playgrounds she was completely at ease, and participated quickly and happily in the group's activities.

For a test, I advised the mother not to abruptly leave her at nursery school—up to now her first different new situation. Rather, the mother should remain at the school for several weeks, sitting at the back, but visible to Carla in the room. The teacher agreed, and reported to the mother that gradually day after day, Carla began to participate more with the group. After 2 weeks she was fully involved cheerfully with the group, and the teacher, the mother, and I all agreed that the mother could discontinue sitting in the school. She did and Carla ignored the change. After that, in the mornings she dressed and had breakfast quickly and was ready eagerly to get to school.

With this successful test, I advised the mother that Carla was a perfectly normal child and that she was an adequate parent. Carla had only the problem of not adjusting quickly to any new situation; she should be called shy. I told the mother to expect that Carla would probably show this same behavioral pattern at any new setting—distressed at first, but with time she would adjust and cheerfully participate. Any special therapy was certainly unnecessary.

Sadly, I have seen all too many cases when a normal child's behavior that was different from the average was labeled pathological in accordance with one of the standard theories, which routinely blamed the parent as being at fault. The child suffered without proper help, the parent was tortured with guilt, and a prolonged expensive therapy was completely wasteful.

3

THE INITIAL HYPOTHESIS

The standard theories were insufficient explanations in so many of our cases. Something must have been missing in those concepts. We puzzled over this problem for many months in the early 1950s.

Then, one day, as we puzzled, we came up with a brand new insight. Maybe the standard theories didn't make sense because many individual differences in the children themselves played an important role in their healthy or deviant development—and not merely the mother's influence. Many references in the professional literature had observations of such differences, but those comments were usually only casual, and no one had attempted to study such individual differences with any serious and systematic effort.

But this new idea was only the first step. Yes, we agreed that individual differences were important in development. But the next question was *how*. How did these differences explain how they were important? We were faced with this unanswered question, and somehow had to find the answer. Suddenly, totally unexpectedly, the answer came from a report of one of my (S.C.) clinical cases.

One evening in 1952 we attended a monthly local professional meeting, and I was scheduled to present an interesting case description. I picked a case that was rather unusual.

13

A CASE PRESENTATION

The boy, Allen, had a troubling behavior problem. Upon meeting the parents at my office, I was struck by how tall they both were. Allen was quite tall also. While he read quietly in the waiting room, his parents sat in my office and poured out their anguish and helplessness at Allen's behavior. In response to my questions, I found out there had been normal pregnancy, birth, and early childhood development. Allen was bright, cooperative, friendly with the neighborhood children, athletic, behaved well in school, and enjoyed learning. But as he grew older he became extraordinarily sensitive to any minor error, mistake, or criticism. If he missed a basketball shot, he immediately considered himself a failure and quit his team. If he engaged in a special academic project, he would be absorbed in the activity until the teacher pointed out a minor error in his work. Then he immediately dropped the project. And so, over and over again, such incidents occurred. Each time the parents and teachers reassured Allen that the minor error was insignificant and that he was actually functioning in his game or project at a high level. But this didn't help; Allen always insisted that he had made a terrible mistake.

As they related this story, the parents, especially the mother, kept repeating to me that they must have been responsible for Allen's behavior. "It must have been our fault," the mother repeated. "Please help us find our mistake."

I questioned them in detail, but couldn't find evidence of the parents' unhealthy behavior or attitudes toward Allen. They were thoughtful, intelligent, and deeply attached to him. There was no evidence of their responsibility for any of Allen's disturbances. In addition, his younger brother showed no evidence of any of his abnormal behavior. By the end of my intensive inquiry, I was still puzzled. My next step was to ask Allen to engage with me in play and discuss his various interests in my playroom. I invited him in. Quickly and quietly he responded with no opposition. Although I knew Allen was only 9 years old, I was again struck by the fact that his height, maturity, and language skills made him seem several years older.

In the playroom, Allen noticed a group of toy automobiles and a stoplight sitting on a large table. Happily, he began to play with the cars. Then, suddenly, by mistake Allen pushed one car through the red signal light. He stopped, looked very unhappy, and in a disturbed manner began to push the cars around helter-skelter so as to make the cars produce one accident after another. Then he ran back to the waiting room.

In this brief incident in the playroom, Allen's behavior matched his parents' description. At that point, I understood a possible explanation for Allen's actions and feelings. To confirm my explanation, I asked the parents some key questions: When Allen was a young child playing with other young children, what had the pattern of play been? Had the parents complained about Allen's behavior? With that I hit the jackpot. The parents immediately described one vivid example after another. The story was typical: A mother would run to Allen's mother to complain that he had just pulled away a toy and pushed "the baby." On one occasion he was scolded by the other child's mother, "Your mother should teach a big boy like you to behave with tiny children." Allen's mother was embarrassed and asked the mother how old the other child was. Allen, it turned out, was actually year younger than "the baby" but appeared much older because of his height and advanced language. Therefore, Allen always got the blame for any upset between children of the same age as or younger than himself.

I asked what happened as Allen grew older. His parents affirmed this same distressing sequence year after year. Other parents would scold Allen: "You are a ruffian and a bully and should be ashamed of picking on a younger kid." They would also complain to his parents because this big, supposedly older boy had hit hard a small younger boy. Allen's parents usually couldn't affect the growing community opinion that he was a menace. His parents tried to reassure and support Allen, but the community group opinion overwhelmed their attempts.

Rejecting the stereotyped psychoanalytic theory that the parents, particularly the mother, was to blame, I emphasized that Allen's problem wasn't their fault. I told them that some or even many children developed behavior problems because they had one or another special intrinsic characteristics that prevented them from coping with the expectations of the family or community. Such children could then fail to adopt the adults' expectations, which could create excessive stress and self-mistrust and finally lead to behavior problems. I proposed that the parents didn't need treatment but rather an explanation of how Allen's special characteristics—his appearance and verbal maturity—were the key to his problems. Advising the parents to reassure Allen and tell him what had been happening, I took him into a course of play psychotherapy. Gradually Allen learned to overcome his expectations that any error could be a disaster. As he grew in insight, he finally conquered his severe behavior problem.

A REVELATION

When S.C. finished this case presentation, the chairperson said politely, "Thank you, that was an interesting case." I said nothing, but I was literally stunned. As I listened to S.C.'s case history, it was for me (A.T.), with no exaggeration, a revelation. S.C.'s story had pointed out what was missing in our psychoanalytic and clinical training. If a child developed a behavior problem, it might not always be the parents' fault. In some cases the child had some special individual characteristics and could not cope with the expectations of the parents or the community or both. Expectations that were inappropriate for the child's specific traits would create stress and anxiety, which could cause some kind of behavior problem. While I sat and considered the exciting implications of my revelation, the audience members were discussing S.C.'s case in all the standard ways—maybe the mother had rejected her son because of conflicts about the second child, or perhaps the mother's unconscious guilt had been transferred to the infant's psyche, etc., etc. Nonsense, I thought, as I absorbed the impact of S.C.'s profound insight, though she had not, at the moment, recognized the full implications of her case report.

After the meeting, we talked for days, and our new basic concept began to be clear. Parents were different from their children, and children in the same family were different from each other. The parents' handling and the child's individual differences would be healthy if their differences were harmonious. If their differences were discordant, then such differences could result in an unhealthy child development. And there might be all kinds of differences in children.

Although we didn't start out to prove it, we felt strongly that these individual differences in children were probably biological in origin. Then we decided that the proof of our concept required a systematic longitudinal study to demonstrate the influence of children's significant differences from early infancy going on to later childhood and even adulthood. Now we faced the formidable task of developing a systematic method of collecting the necessary information. First we thought of some biological method because we believed from the evidence that people had a biological basis for individual differences, which were present from the newborn period on.

We spoke to a brilliant neurophysiologist we knew, explained our search for a method of investigating the question, and asked if he could help us. He understood, thought, and then laughed, "It is too tough a problem. I'm glad it's your problem, not mine."

4

THE FIRST RESEARCH EFFORT: FROM FAILURE TO SUCCESS

Our first attempt was to prove that infants had specific individual differences in conditioning; a distinctly Pavlovian neurologic model. To do this we needed a group of cooperative mothers in their last weeks of pregnancy. Fortunately, one of our friends was pregnant, soon to deliver, and she and her husband were fascinated by our idea. They volunteered and enlisted about six other families who were expecting babies. As the mothers notified us when they delivered, I (S.C.) went to the hospital and gave each mother a small tinkling bell, a stopwatch, and a ruled time chart. The mother's process was clear: When the baby was hungry and cried, the mother rang the bell and gave the baby the milk. For the next few times when the baby started to cry, the mother rang the bell, started the stopwatch, and recorded how long until the baby stopped crying and then how long until it started to cry again. We were trying to gauge babies' different responses to the bell ringing after they had had the experience of feeding after the bell rang.

I telephoned every mother each day. Soon, it became obvious that the conditioning procedure of the babies didn't work. Our first research strategy was a failure. The baby wasn't obliging by stopping its crying at the sound of the bell. But as I listened to the mothers I realized that I was getting more data. Each mother had no problem describing her own behavior and that of her baby during this conditioning experiment. We continued to chat about anything else the mother was interested in describing about her child's behavior. After several discussions with these mothers, I began spontaneously to ask specific questions on the infant's sleep schedule, behavior with feeding, diapering, bathing, and so on. I realized that with these data I could get a vivid picture, an internal videotape in my mind, about each baby's behavior. And they were all different—sometimes dramatically different.

I told A.T. what was happening and said, "Let's forget about conditioning; that hasn't worked. But now I can get a very clear picture of each child's behavior from the mothers' reports. And each baby is different. So, let's make sure we work out a way of creating clear descriptions from the mother of all the items the child does—sleeping, feeding, bathing, dressing, and so on. We won't let the mother just give general statements but will always ask for specific descriptions. It will be almost as good as being next to the child. This will be naturalistic behavior. There won't be a stranger hanging around, which might change the child's and mother's behavior."

A.T. stared at me. "What's the matter?" I asked him. "Stella, your idea is so brilliant, it's so clear. It provides a way of finding detailed and specific data on individual differences in children. We have struggled for years and now you have found the answer. Our first attempt involved a search for scientific data through conditioning or some as yet unknown biological data. Now you have found the answer, by gathering specific detailed and empirical behavioral descriptions of the child's routine daily activities, plus information on any special incidents whenever they might occur."

We now possessed a method for obtaining the data we needed through systematic and objective questioning of the parents—the unique source of information of their children's behavior. Parents are actively involved with their children day to day, even hour to hour, from infancy to later childhood. Also, they are knowledgeable about the details of their child's response to any special event or unexpected incident. The alternative research method would be to have a trained observer spend a variable period of time in the home recording the details of the child's behavior. But the use of such an observer was expensive, and even more important, was inadequate. Unless the observer actually lived in the family's home for months, he or she would miss important items of the child's behavioral responses to unscheduled or unpredictable events.

5

THE NEW YORK LONGITUDINAL STUDY (NYLS)

Step-by-step we decided that the individual differences of children played some important role in their healthy or deviant development. We then formulated a promising theory as to the actual significance of these differences in the child–environment interaction, and developed a specific and practical research strategy for gathering the details of the individual behavioral characteristics of children.

Now that we had come to this point, we were ready to go ahead with launching a complex anterospective longitudinal study. Such a study is laborious and time-consuming, and one must wait for definitive findings. A longitudinal study also represents a gamble! For example, if it becomes clear when the subjects are 10 years old that certain information from age 1 or 2 is crucial, it is too late to go back and get this information reliably, or even at all.

However, for our purpose there was no substitute for a longitudinal study for tracing the histories of the children over time. Child A might be high in a particular rating at 2 years and low at 5, and child B the reverse—low at 2 years and high at 5 years. Only a longitudinal study that followed each child over time would be able to detect such individual shifts, which might be crucial to the understanding of the differences in the psychological development of children.

In such a longitudinal study, it would also be vital that the questions of the interviews should be focused on the current or recent age period of the children. Such a method, called anterospective, minimizes the danger that the parents will distort the accuracy of the child's behavior as time fades recollections (Wenar, 1963).

THE PARENTAL INTERVIEW PROTOCOLS

We constructed a detailed outline in order to obtain both background and behavioral information. Background included sibs, parental occupations, brief obstetrical and neonatal history, responsibilities for the daily care of the infant, and parental description of the child's personality. This last question was not asked to obtain objective data, but as a possible clue to parental attitudes. It was asked in a nondirective manner, as an open-ended question.

The detailed behaviors of daily living were categorized and itemized: sleep and feeding schedules, new foods, soiling and wetting, bathing, nail cutting, hair brushing, visits to the doctor, dressing and undressing, reactions to sensory stimuli, motility, responses to people, response to illness, and pattern of crying. The questions for each items were specific objective questions. As a typical example, under "bathing," the following questions were asked: At what age was the first bath given, and how did the baby react? Was there a change from this reaction during subsequent baths? If so, was this a gradual or an abrupt change? Did the baby behave differently in different bathtubs or if the bath was given by a different person? For any parental answer to any question, we were not satisfied with a general answer. Thus:

Q. How did the baby react to the first bath?

A. She loved it.
Q. Can you specify what "loved it" meant. Did the baby smile, coo, or laugh, sit quietly or splash?
   Or
Q. How did the baby react to the first bath?
A. He hated it.
Q. Can you specify what "hated it" meant. Did the baby fuss or cry loudly, hold his body stiffly, or squirm?

We also asked what the parents did with this negative reaction. Did they try to soothe the baby, distract him with a toy, or take him out immediately? What did they do to get the baby to accept the bath? Did they put the baby in the tub on subsequent days, or only after skipping several days or more, and how long did it take the baby to show pleasure while in the bath? Again, did the baby smile and coo or laugh, sit quietly or splash?

This same sequence of questioning was used for all the routines of living. This elicited specific detailed and objective descriptions of the baby's behavior. Also, we had indirect but important clues as to the parent's pattern of child-care behavior.

We paid special attention to the details of the child's first behavior at any environmental change, such as a move to another house or apartment, and we traced the specific changes in behavior required, if any, to adapt to such a change.

COLLECTION OF NYLS SAMPLE

The initial sample was gathered through personal contact during pregnancy or shortly after birth. These parents then referred their friends and relatives, who were interested in the nature of our study. Only one mother who was approached refused to participate. All resided in New York City or one of the suburbs. This method of contact resulted in families of native-born middle- or upper-middle-class background.

The cumulative collection of subjects was started in March 1956, and completed over a 6-year period. Eighty-seven families were enrolled, and all children born to the families during the 6-year period were included in the study. The total initial sample comprised 138 children, with 47 families contributing one child each, 31 contributing two children, 7 contributing three children, and 2 with four children.

The homogeneous sociocultural nature of this sample was an advantage to our project. Our aim was the study of the characteristics and functional importance of individual behavioral differences in the children's development. If our sample had included a mixed heterogeneous sociocultural group, this would have introduced special variables that would have complicated and even confused our analyses of our primary aim of the data collection. We did take this issue into account by initiating and following a separate longitudinal study of 95 children of unskilled or semiskilled working-class Puerto Rican parents, with data protocol and analytic strategy methods identical with the NYLS. This enabled us to identify significant sociocultural differences shaped by a comparison of the findings of the two longitudinal studies. (These and other cultural influences of temperament are reported in Chapter 23).

MAINTENANCE OF THE NYLS SAMPLE

Maintenance of sample over time is a crucial issue in any longitudinal study. If any significant degree of sample attrition were to occur, there would be no satisfactory method of determining whether those subjects lost to the study had any specific characteristics that would have altered the results of data analysis. To minimize this danger of sample attrition, we developed a number of guidelines that were meticulously followed by our staff and ourselves. Only five children from five families were lost to the NYLS study in the first 3 years due to long-distance changes in residence. Our resources at that time were insufficient to continue active contact with families outside the New York City area. With our additional resources in subsequent years, no further attrition occurred until the subjects were in their early twenties, even though the families had been characterized by a great deal of geographical mobility. In our last follow-up, when they were in their middle and late twenties, we lost only four subjects, for idiosyncratic reasons.

THE COLLECTION OF DATA

Originally, we explored the possibility of obtaining behavioral data from the neonatal period and onward. A pilot study showed that in the first few weeks or a month, behavior varied substantially from day to day, and that data collection and analysis would be an exceedingly demanding and complex process. This is not to negate the existence of behavioral individuality in the neonate, which has been documented by a number of workers (Brazelton, 1973; Korner, 1973). It may be that this inconsistency of behavior is due, in the first weeks, to residual maternal hormones in the infant's blood or that the neonate's physiological instability is due to the process of delivery.

Further exploration indicated that, in general, the infant's behavioral characteristics usually began to show definiteness and consistency of patterning between the fourth and eight weeks of life. Hence, we started our parental interviews at 2 to 3 months. During the first 18 months of the child's life, the interviews were scheduled every 3 months, then every 6 months until 5 years of age, and thereafter yearly until 7 to 8 years. At each age stage, the range of questions was expanded to include the new maturational behavioral capacities.

During those age periods, additional information was obtained by school observations and teacher interviews, and IQ tests and behavioral observations of the child's responses to the IQ items at ages 3 and 6 years. In addition, when the child reached the age of 3 years, a special structured interview was used to elicit detailed information on parental opinions on their own attitudes and caretaking techniques. Also included were parental recollections of age and manner of occurrence of specific events such as toilet training. Each parent was interviewed simultaneously but in separate rooms, and, with permission, these interviews were tape-recorded for later transcription and analysis. Because of limitation of funding in sequential child age-periods, follow-ups were restricted to the clinical evaluation of subjects showing evidence of behavior disorder. When funding expanded, most of the parents and the subjects themselves were interviewed when the subjects were 16 years old, again when they were 18 to 22 years old, and finally were in their mid- and late twenties. New interviews were still ongoing into their late thirties.

CLINICAL EVALUATION

Inasmuch as a primary objective of the NYLS involved the influences of individual behavioral differences on the development and evaluation of either normal development or behavior disorders, special attention was paid to ensure that each case with evidence of behavior deviation was identified by our parental and/or teacher reports and fully evaluated clinically. Almost all the psychiatric evaluation in childhood and adolescence were made by S.C. and by A.T. when the subjects reached adulthood. In a few cases, the parents themselves saw other psychiatrists and reports were obtained from them.

Special sensory, neurological, or psychological studies were undertaken when a youngster's history and the psychiatric findings suggested such a need.

Following the clinical evaluation, its findings were reviewed along with the data of the previous parental interviews, school observations and teacher interviews, and
the psychometric reports. A dynamic formulation of the
child—environment interactions responsible for the behavioral deviations was formulated, and a final diagnosis
made. Then one of us met with the parents, explained the
reasons for the child's behavior, and made recommendations for management. The dynamic formulation of the
child's problem and the recommendations made to the
parents are detailed in Chapters 8 and 9. During the subjects' adolescence there were parental requests for psychiatric consultation. These were done by the authors, if the
youngster found this acceptable, and final discussion was
held with parents and adolescent either together or separately. In a few situations, the young person's viewpoint
appeared more valid than that of the parents. In young
adulthood, requests for consultation came from the subjects themselves and were always honored as a responsibility of the conduct of the study.

THE ACCURACY OF PARENTAL INTERVIEWS

We had devised a method of recording detailed, meaningful information about each child's own behavior. We
were then faced with the question: How accurate were
the parents' reports? Our technique of avoiding parental
distortions had three main directions. First, we had indicated to the parents that the children's individual differences were basically normal. There was no need to worry
that they were describing their children's behavior in
some unfavorable, unhealthy light. Second, we pressed
the parents to describe objective, factual actions either in
place of, or to illustrate, subjective interpretation. For example, if a parent said, "My child is unhappy," we asked
for a description of the details of the child's behavior that
illustrated the statement "unhappy." By the time the de-

tailed behavior was elicited, it became clear that the child was very unhappy, mildly unhappy, or not unhappy at all. Third, the interval between interviews was every 3 months during the first 18 months when change and development in the child proceeded rapidly. Then, until age 3, the interval was every 6 months, and after that once a year.

Furthermore, to check the parents' accuracy, two trained observers who did not know the families went separately to the homes of 18 subjects and took detailed notes of their behavior over a 2- to 3-hour period. Their observations showed a significant positive correlation with the mothers' reports. Finally, because almost all the interviews were performed in the families' homes, there were many opportunities to watch the child's behavior unobtrusively, and a close correlation was found with what the parents were reporting.

Finally, our finding that parents can give accurate reports of their children's behavior has been confirmed by other researchers (Costello, 1975; Dunn & Kendrick, 1980; Wilson & Matheny, 1983). As an example, a comment by two respected and experienced research psychologists, Weisz and Sigman (1993), emphasized that "assessing parent reports may be a particularly useful first step because (1) parents have a particularly comprehensive observational base, that is, more exposure to the child across more settings than say teachers or trained observers, (2) parents may have somewhat better descriptive language skills than their children, and (3) parent reports reflect the combination of actual child behavior and culturally influenced perception that is the essence of 'child problems' in the first place." They have reinforced our findings with their more elegant prose.

6

ANALYSIS OF DATA AND THE DEFINITION AND RATING OF TEMPERAMENT AND CATEGORIES

After the first round of parental interviews covering the first 12 months with 22 children—we had 80 interviews that had been done at 3-month intervals and were faced with organizing this mountain of data into specific categories and rating them. We were clinicians who had not been trained in techniques for analyzing research data. Fortunately we had a friend, Dr. Herbert G. Birch, who had a truly brilliant talent for investigating and systematically analyzing data from animal and child research studies. We persuaded Herb Birch to develop a system of categories and ratings from our voluminous data. With a true tour de force, by 1959, he had established nine categories of behavioral individuality definitions and a method of rating them by an induction content analysis.

Dr. Michael Rutter, a young, promising psychiatrist, became intrigued by our concept and data, questioning the significance of behavioral individuality of children on their development. He received a British Fellowship in 1962 to study the activities of research studies in the United States and elected to spend 6 months of the fellowship working with us and Dr. Birch on our NYLS data. At the time, we had coined the term "primary reaction patterns" to label individual behaviorality. We were not happy with the term. It was clumsy and vague. What did "primary" and "reaction" mean? Rutter also criticized the term, but he had an immediate answer: "The word 'temperament' is a simple, meaningful term, it has been used professionally over the ages, and we should use it, not 'primary reaction pattern.' " We immediately agreed, accepted the term temperament and, along with Herbert Birch and Michael Rutter, spelled out its detailed definition. Over the years, Dr. Rutter, has been recognized internationally as a leading child psychiatrist, and recently has been knighted by the British government because of the significance of his professional work.

DEFINITION OF TEMPERAMENT

Temperament may best be viewed as a general term referring to the *how* of behavior. It differs from ability, which is concerned with the *what* and *how well* of behaving, and from motivation, which accounts for *why* a person does what he or she is doing. Temperament, by contrast, concerns the *way* in which an individual behaves. Two children may dress themselves with equal skillfulness or ride a bicycle with the same dexterity and have the same motives for engaging in these activities. Two adolescents may display similar learning ability and intellectual interest, and their academic goals may coincide. Two adults may show the same technical expertness in their work and have the same reason for devoting themselves to their jobs. Yet, these two children, adolescents, or adults may differ significantly with regard to the quickness with which they move; the ease with which they approach a new physical environment, social situation, or task; the intensity and character of their mood expression; and the effort required by others to distract them when they are absorbed in an activity.

Temperament can be equated to the term "behavioral style." Each refers to the *how* rather than the *what* (abilities and content) or the *why* (motivations) of behavior. In this definition, temperament is a phenomenological term and has no implications as to etiology or immutability. Like any other characteristic of the organism—whether it be height, weight, intellectual competence, perceptual skills—temperament is influenced by environmental factors in its expression and even in its nature as development proceeds.

THE NINE CATEGORIES

When Dr. Birch established the nine categories, we reviewed them with him and had several minor changes for the terms, with which he agreed. We had ourselves defined a number of the categories as we did the parental interviews, and some of Dr. Birch's nine categories corresponded, but his definitions were more precise than ours, and we had overlooked several of his categories. The categories made sense for the three of us for the practical implications of the meaningful characteristics of a child's behavior. Now using the term "temperament," we reported this analysis of the nine categories of temperament, their definitions and their ratings.

1. Activity level. The motor component present in a given child's functioning and the diurnal proportion of active and inactive periods.

2. Rhythmicity (regularity). The predictability and/or unpredictability in time of any function. It can be analyzed in relation to the sleep-wake cycle, hunger, feeding pattern, and elimination schedule.

3. Approach or withdrawal. The nature of the initial response to a new stimulus, be it a new food, a new toy, or a new person. Approach responses are positive, whether displayed by mood expression (smiling, verbalizations, and the like) or motor activity (swallowing a new food, reaching for a new toy, active play, and so on). Withdrawal reactions are negative, whether displayed by mood expression (crying, fussing, grimacing, verbalizations, or the like) or motor activity (moving away, spitting new food out, pushing new toy away, and so forth).

4. Adaptability. Responses to new or altered situations. One is not concerned with the nature of the initial responses, but rather the ease with which they are modified in a desired direction.

5. Threshold of responsiveness. The intensity level of stimulation that is necessary to evoke a discernible response, irrespective of the specific form that the response may take, or the sensory modality affected. The behaviors utilized are those concerning reactions to sensory stimuli, environmental objects, and social contacts.

6. Intensity of reaction. The energy level of response, irrespective of its quality or direction.

7. Quality of mood. The amount of pleasant, joyful, and friendly behavior, as contrasted with unpleasant, crying, and unfriendly behavior.

8. Distractibility. The effectiveness of extraneous environmental stimuli in interfering with or in altering the direction of the ongoing behavior.

9. Attention span and persistence. Two categories that are related. Attention span concerns the length of time a particular activity is pursued by the child. Persistence refers to the continuation of an activity in the face of obstacles to the maintenance of the activity direction.

THE RATINGS OF THE CATEGORIES

The ratings of each category were obtained by item scoring. Each separate item of objective behavior was scored on a 3-point scale: high, medium, or low. To avoid contamination by halo effects, each protocol was scored for one category at a time, and no successive interviews of a given child were scored contiguously. A simplified quantitative *weighted rating* score was obtained for each category for each subject. For the item scoring of any category, each item of mild was scored as 0, medium as 1, and high as 2. The total scores were added, then the total items divided, and a final score obtained. For example, the item scores of a category were totaled as 5 zeros (0), 7 ones (7), and 8 twos (16). These numbers (0 + 7 + 16) added to 23. The total number of items was 5 + 7 + 8, and added to 20. The item scores (23) were divided by the total items (20), resulting in a weighted score of 1.15. This calculation produced a score that took into account all the items of the category for the subject—mild, moderate, and severe.

THE THREE TEMPERAMENT CONSTELLATIONS

Beyond the identification of the nine categories, as the two of us interviewed the parents, we became impressed, even convinced, that the behavioral characteristics of some of the children showed one or another of three special constellations. These were not new categories beyond the nine categories, but clusters of several of the categories that appeared functionally significant.

The first group is characterized by regularity, positive approach responses to new stimuli, high adaptability to change, and mild or moderately intense mood that is preponderantly positive. These children quickly develop regular sleep and feeding schedules, take to most new foods easily, smile at strangers, adapt easily to a new school, accept most frustrations with little fuss, and accept the rules of new games with no trouble. Such a youngster is aptly called the easy child, and is usually a joy to parents, pediatricians, and teachers. The group comprises about 40% of our NYLS sample.

At the opposite end of the temperamental spectrum is the group with irregularity in biological function, negative withdrawal responses to new stimuli, nonadaptability to change, and intense mood expressions that are frequently negative. These children show irregular sleep and feeding schedules, slow acceptance of new foods, prolonged adjustment periods to new routines, people, or situations, and relatively frequent and loud periods of crying. Laughter also is characteristically loud. Frustration typically produces a violent tantrum. This is the difficult child, and mothers and pediatricians find such youngsters difficult indeed. This group comprises about 10% of our NYLS sample.

Some objections have been raised to the term "difficult temperament," because the term "difficult" tends to have a negative connotation and overlooks the positive aspects that a difficult child may actually show as invaluable elements of behavior. The terms "feisty" and "spirited" temperament, which suggest positive attributes, have been suggested. These terms are useful, for it is necessary to recognize that a difficult child is perfectly normal. However, the term difficult temperament is mostly used, because it has been established in temperament research and literature.

A weighted score for easy or difficult temperament for each subject was obtained by one continuous score by a summation of the weighted scores for the five categories of those two constellations (regularity, approach withdrawal, adaptability, mood, and intensity), and divided by 5. A high weighted score that included low intensity identified an easy child. A low weighted score that included high intensity identified a difficult child.

The third noteworthy temperamental constellation is marked by a combination of negative responses of mild intensity to new stimuli with slow adaptability after repeated contact. In contrast to the difficult children, these youngsters are characterized by mild intensity of reactions, whether positive or negative, and by less tendency to show irregularity of biological functions. The negative mild responses to new stimuli can be seen in the first encounter with the bath, a new food, a stranger, a new place, or a new school situation. If given the opportunity to reexperience such new situations over time and without pressure, such a child gradually comes to show quiet and positive interest and involvement. A youngster with this characteristic sequence of response is referred to as the "slow-to-warm-up child," an apt if inelegant designation. About 15% of our NYLS sample falls into this category.

A weighted score for this constellation was calculated by obtaining the same calculation of easy versus difficult temperament, with two exceptions. The continuum of the five high weighted scores for difficult temperament, excluding regularity and high intensity, was substituted by low intensity. In other words, a slow-to-warm-up child was identified with scores similar to those of a difficult child, except that irregularity was excluded and intensity was mild to moderate, but not high.

As can be seen from the above percentages, not all children fit into one of these three temperamental groups. This results from the varying and different combinations of temperamental traits that are manifested by individual children. Also, among those children who do fit one of these three patterns, there is a wide range in degree of manifestation. Some are extremely easy children in practically all situations; others are relatively easy and not always so. A few children are extremely difficult with all new situations and demands; others show only some of these characteristics and relatively mildly. For some children it is highly predictable that they will warm up slowly in any new situation; others warm up slowly with certain types of new stimuli or demands, but warm up quickly in others.

It should be emphasized that the various temperamental constellations all represent variations within normal limits. Any child may be easy, difficult, or slow-to-warm-up temperamentally, have a high or low activity level, distractibility and low persistence or the opposite, or any other relatively extreme rating score in a sample of children for a specific temperamental attribute. However, such an amodal rating is not a criterion of psychopathology, but rather an indication of the wide range of behavioral styles exhibited by normal children.

The body of the NYLS quantitative scores of the nine temperamental categories for each of the first 5 years of life was subject to factor analyses to determine whether meaningful groupings of the categories could be derived statistically. The Varimax solutions proved to be most useful, and three factors were developed. One of these, Factor A, met the criterion of relative consistency over the 5-year period. This factor included approach/withdrawal, adaptability, mood, and intensity. The scores for Factor A were normally distributed for each of the 5 years.

It is significant that the cluster of characteristics constituting Factor A corresponds closely to the cluster developed by qualitative analysis that identifies the easy child and the difficult child. In this qualitative categorization, which was completed *before* the factor analysis was done, the easy child corresponds to high Factor A plus regularity, and the difficult child to low Factor A plus irregularity.

TEMPERAMENT QUESTIONNAIRES

Our first NYLS professional publication on temperament appeared in 1957. Over the years, other research and clinical mental health professionals became interested in our reports of our systematic structure of temperament categories and their ratings. An important problem arose; our protocols for data collection and rating were time-consuming. Shorter methods were required for the many studies related to temperament. In 1970, a pediatrician, Dr. William Carey, working with a psychologist, Dr. Sean McDevitt, devised a short parental questionnaire for infancy temperament based on our NYLS categories and definitions (Carey, 1970). This questionnaire was quickly adapted and widely utilized over time for its usefulness in research and clinical studies. The employment of this time-saving questionnaire stimulated the development of temperament questionnaires for various age periods in childhood (Carey, 1986), adolescence (Lerner, Palermo, Spiro, & Nesselrode, 1982), and early adulthood (Thomas et al., 1982).

Some researchers have developed modifications of our temperament categories, or even altered them. But, by now, the studies of the individual differences of childhood—different national, class, and cultural characteristics, cognitive levels, and developmental deviations—have been shown to stand up well with our basic temperament categories and ratings.

7

THE CLINICAL
INTERVIEW FOR
TEMPERAMENT

We have provided a relatively short clinical interview
for parents. This usually required 20 to 30 minutes, less
time than a questionnaire, but more informative for a clinician.

An accurate diagnostic judgment requires that data on
the child's temperamental characteristics be gathered
with the same care and regard for detail that are considered essential for the evaluation of parental attitudes and
practices, family relationships, and sociocultural influences. Naturally, clinicians do not have anterospectively
gathered behavioral descriptions of a child's developmental course available to them. But neither do they have
available such anterospective data on intra- and extrafamilial environmental influences. With all information
gathered retrospectively, whether it be on temperament,
the attainment of developmental landmarks, the medical
history, the patterns of parental functioning, or special
environmental events, clinicians must assess the accuracy, completeness, and pertinence of the data reported
to them. In the authors' experience, the collection of behavioral data from which evaluations of temperament can
be made has presented no greater difficulties than has

gathering information on other aspects of the clinical history. Some informants are able to give detailed, factual, and precise descriptions of their children's past and present behavior. Others give vague, general, and subjective reports. In all cases, it is desirable to confirm the accuracy of the data by directly observing the child and, wherever possible, by obtaining information from multiple sources.

A number of items in the basic clinical history, such as the course of the child's development and the history of the presenting complaints, will often in themselves elicit clues as to significant issues relating to the child's temperament. For example, the parents of a 12-year-old boy reported that he was unable to study or do homework at an academic level appropriate to his intellectual capacity and his grade placement, and that he started many endeavors, such as music lessons or rock collections, but seemed to lose interest in them rapidly. The parents also complained that routines took an inordinate amount of time to be accomplished, although the child was cheerful and apparently well-intentioned. He would start on his way to bed but might be found 15 minutes later puttering with some game that attracted his attention, playing with a brother, or involved in a discussion with his grandmother. The composite of presenting problems in this case suggested that the temperamental quality of distractibility might be an important factor in causing the child's difficulties.

As another example, the parents of a 9-year-old girl reported that she found it difficult to undertake new endeavors and to join new groups of children her own age and that she tended to avoid new situations whenever she could. This presenting complaint suggested the possibility that a temperamentally based tendency to make initial withdrawal reactions to new experiences might be relevant to the reported behavioral difficulty.

Following the taking of a basic clinical history, systematic inquiry can be made into the child's temperamental characteristics during infancy, keeping in mind the necessity to investigate similarly other possible causes for the problem behaviors. The inquiry can be started with the general question, "After you brought the baby home from the hospital and in the first few weeks and months of his life, what was he or she like?"

First answers to such questions are usually very general ones: "He was wonderful." "He cried day and night." "She was a bundle of nerves." "She was a joy."

The next question, "Would you give me some details that will describe what you mean?" is still open-ended.

The replies to the second general question often include useful descriptions of behaviors from which judgments of temperament can be made. Further information requires specific inquiry, which is most economically pursued by asking questions about behavior relevant to defining each of the temperamental attributes, one at a time. The questions asked should be directed at obtaining a number of descriptive behavioral items from which the interviewer can then make an estimate of the child's temperamental characteristics. A list of questions appropriate to each of the new categories are suggested in the following section.

QUESTIONS FOR THE CLINICAL INTERVIEW

Activity Level

How much did your baby move around? Did he move around a lot, was he very quiet, or somewhere in between? If you put him to bed for a nap and it took him 10 or 15 minutes to fall asleep, would you have to go in to rearrange the covers, or would he be lying so quietly that you know they would be in their proper place and not disarranged? If you were changing her diaper and discovered that you had left the powder just out of reach, could you safely dash over to get it and come right back without worrying that she would flip over the surface and fall? Did you have trouble changing her diaper, pulling her shirt over her head, or putting on any other clothes because she wiggled about, or could you count on her lying quietly to be dressed?

Rhythmicity

How did you arrange the baby's feedings? Could you tell by the time he was 6 weeks (2 months, 3 months) old about when during the day he would be hungry, sleepy, or wake up? Could you count on this happening about the same time every day or did the baby vary from day to day? If he varied, how marked was it? When during the day did he have his bowel movements (time and number) and was this routine, variable, or predictable?

Parents can generally recall such events. They will say, "She was as regular as clockwork"; "I could never figure out when to start a long job because one day she would have a long nap and the next day she wouldn't sleep more than 15 minutes"; or, "I used to try to take her out for her airing after I cleaned her from her bowel movement, but I never could figure it right because her time changed every day."

Adaptability

How would you describe the way the child responded to changed circumstances? For example, when he was shifted from a bathinette to a bathtub, if he didn't take to the change immediately, could you count on his getting used to the tub quickly or did it take a long time? (Parents should be asked to define what they mean by "quickly" and what they mean by "a long time" in terms of days or weeks.) If her first reaction to a new person was a negative one, how long did it take the child to become familiar with the person? If she didn't like a new food the first time it was offered, could you count on her getting to like it and most other new foods sooner or later? If so, how long would it take if the new food was offered to her daily or several times a week?

Approach/ Withdrawal

How did the baby behave with new events, such as when given his first tub bath, offered new foods, or taken care of by a new person for the first time? Did he fuss, did he do nothing, or did he seem to like it? Were there any changes during her infancy that you remember, such as a shift to a new bed, a visit to a new place, or a permanent move? Describe the child's initial behavior at these times.

Threshold Level

How would you estimate the baby's sensitivity to noises, to heat and cold, to things he saw and tasted, and to textures of clothing? Did he seem to be very aware of or unresponsive to these things? For example, did you have to tiptoe about when the baby was sleeping lest he be awakened? If he heard a faint noise while awake, would he tend to notice the sound by looking toward it? Did bright lights or bright sunshine make him blink or cry? Did the baby's behavior seem to show that she noticed the difference when a familiar person wore glasses or a new hairstyle for the first time in her presence? If she didn't like a new food and an old food that she liked very much was put with it on the spoon, would the baby still notice the taste of the new one and reject it? Did you have to be careful about clothing you put on her because some textures were too rough? If so, describe the kind of things she disliked.

Intensity of Reaction

How did you know when the baby was hungry? Did he squeak, did he roar, or were his sounds somewhere in between? How could you tell that he didn't like a food?

Did he just quietly turn his head away from the spoon or did he start crying loudly? If you held her hand to cut her fingernails and she didn't like it, did she fuss a little or a lot? If she liked something, did she usually smile and coo or did she laugh loudly? In general, would you say she let her pleasure or displeasure be known loudly or softly?

Quality of Mood

How could you tell when the baby liked something or disliked something? After a description of the infant's behavior in these respects is obtained, the parents should be asked if the infant was more often contented or more often discontented and on what basis they made this judgment.

Distractibility

If the child was in the midst of sucking on a bottle or breast, would he stop what he was doing if he heard a sound or if another person came by, or would he continue sucking? If she was hungry and fussing or crying while the bottle was being warmed, could you divert her easily and stop her crying by holding her or giving her a plaything? If she was playing, for example, gazing at her fingers or using a rattle, would other sights and sounds get her attention very quickly or very slowly?

Persistence and Attention Span

Would you say that the baby usually stuck with something he was doing for a long time or only momentarily? For example, describe the longest time he remained engrossed in an activity all by himself. How old was he and what was he doing? (Examples might be playing with the cradle gym or watching a mobile.) If she reached for something, say a toy in the bathtub, and couldn't get it easily, would she keep after it or give up very quickly?

THE THREE TEMPERAMENTAL CONSTELLATIONS

This identification of the nine categories through the clinical interview has made it possible to also label the three constellations: easy, difficult, or slow-to-warm-up temperament. This can easily be done by clustering the specific categories for each pattern. Thus, a child with irregularity, withdrawal, low adaptability, negative mood, and high intensity can be patterned as difficult temperament, and similar groupings of appropriate categories can likewise identify the easy or slow-to-warm-up temperament.

After completing the inventory of the child's temperamental characteristics in infancy, the next step is to identify those attributes that appear extreme in their manifestations and/or those that seem clearly related to the child's current pattern of deviant behavior. This is followed by an inquiry into the characteristics of these temperament attributes at succeeding age stage periods of development. Thus, if the history of the infancy period suggests a pattern of marked distractibility, it would be desirable to gather data on behavior related to distractibility at succeeding age-periods and in varied life situations, such as play, school, and homework. Similarly, if the presenting complaints indicate that the child currently finds it difficult to undertake new endeavors or to join new groups of age-mates, and if the early temperamental history suggests a characteristic pattern of initial withdrawal coupled with slow adaptation, it would be important to obtain descriptions of the child's patterns of initial responses to situations and demands that arose at different points in the child's developmental course.

The final step in the assessment of the child's temperament is the evaluation of current temperamental characteristics. The behavioral information obtained for current functioning is usually more valid than that obtained for behavioral patterns in the past, since there is less chance of forgetting or of retrospective distortion. The inquiry into current behavior attempts to cover all temperamental categories and concentrates on those that appear most pertinent to the presenting symptoms.

Activity level may be estimated from a child's behavior preferences. Would the child rather sit quietly for a long time engrossed in some task or prefer to seek out opportunities for active physical play? How well does the child fare in routines that require sitting still for extended periods of time? For example, can he or she sit through an entire meal without seeking an opportunity to move about? Must a long train or automobile ride be broken up by frequent stops because of the child's restlessness?

Rhythmicity can be explored through questions about the child's habits and their regularity. For instance, does the child get sleepy at regular and predictable times? Does he or she have any characteristic routines relating to hunger, such as taking a snack immediately after school or during the evening? Are the child's bowel movements regular?

Adaptability can be identified through a consideration of the way the child reacts to changes in environment. Does the child adjust easily and fit quickly into changed family patterns? Does he or she have difficulty adapting to the routines of a new classroom or a new teacher? Is the child willing to go along with other children's preferences or always insist on pursuing only his or her own interests?

Approach/withdrawal, or the youngster's pattern of response to new events or new people, can be explored in many ways. Questions can be directed at the nature of the child's reaction to new clothing, new neighborhood children, a new school, and a new teacher. What is the child's attitude when a family excursion is being planned? Will he or she try new foods or new activities easily or not?

Threshold level is more difficult to explore in an older child than in a young one. However, it is sometimes possible to obtain information on unusual features of threshold such as hypersensitivity or remarkable unresponsiveness to noise, to visual stimuli, or to rough clothing.

The intensity of reactions can be ascertained by finding out how the child displays disappointment or pleasure. If something pleasant happens, does the child tend to be mildly enthusiastic, average in expression of joy, or ecstatic? When the child is unhappy, does he or she fuss quietly or bellow with rage or distress?

Quality of mood can usually be estimated by parental descriptions of their offspring's overall expressions of mood. Is the child predominantly happy and contented or a frequent complainer and more often unhappy than not?

Distractibility, even when not a present problem, will declare itself in the parent's descriptions of ordinary routines. Does the child often start off to do something and then get sidetracked by something a sib is doing, by a coin collection, or by any number of circumstances that catches her eye or ear? Or, on the contrary, once engaged in an activity, is the child impervious to what is going on around him?

Data on persistence and attention span are usually easier to obtain for the older child than for the infant. The degree of persistence in the face of difficulty can be ascertained with regard to games, puzzles, athletic activities, such as learning to ride a bicycle, and schoolwork. Similarly, after the initial difficulty in mastering these activities has been overcome, the length of the child's attention span for and concentration on these same kinds of activities can be ascertained.

In many instances, additional data on temperamental organization can be obtained by querying teachers or other adults familiar with the child's behavior. For such inquiry, the history-taking protocol for the parents can be utilized if it is appropriately modified to permit a focus on the areas of the child's functioning with which the adult is acquainted. Observation of the child's behavior during a clinical play interview or in the course of psychological testing can also supply useful information on activity level, approach/withdrawal, intensity of reactions, quality of mood, distractibility, and persistence and attention span. Temperamental characteristics that require information on the child's behavior over time, namely rhythmicity and adaptability, cannot be made from such single observations over a short time span, and the nature of the clinical observation and testing situations is such that behavior referable to the sensory threshold characteristic of the child is usually not observable.

8

THE CONCEPT OF GOODNESS OF FIT

In following the NYLS subjects, we paid special attention to any of those who developed definite symptoms of behavior disorder. A major purpose of the NYLS project was the exploration of the etiology and dynamics of behavior disorders in children. Hence, when a child showed any specific symptoms of behavior disorders, reported by the parents or the staff interviewer, the subject was referred to one of us (S.C.) for a systematic, comprehensive clinical study of the case, after which a diagnostic judgment and assignment of the degree of the behavioral problem as normal, mild, moderate, or severe was made. The standard criteria, as classified in the third edition of the *Diagnostic and Statistical Manual of Mental Disorders* (DSM-III) of the American Psychiatric Association, was used to specify the type of disorder, for example, adjustment disorder, conduct disorder, depression, brain damage.

The next step required a formulation that included a comprehensive conceptualization of the process of development of the dynamic interplay of the relevant multidimensional factors in specific individuals. The variables that were functionally relevant at a particular age-period were identified, such as, what determined the outcome of the interaction among these variables so that either healthy or pathological development was promoted, how stress and excessive stress were generated and resolved, how anxiety and defense mechanisms were produced and evolved.

To answer these questions, all the NYLS data to date was reviewed in addition to the findings of the clinical examination. In one subject after another, I (S.C.) was struck in most cases by the relevance of the specific nature of the child–parent interactional process. This interactional process challenged the validity of the currently prevalent assumption that a child's problem was a direct reaction to unhealthy maternal influences. In contrast, the interactional events emerging showed a two-way street, in which a child's temperament and other characteristics could influence the parent's attitude and behavior, as much as the parent's functioning could influence the child's behavior. I concluded that parent–child interaction should be analyzed not only for parental influences on the child but equally for the influence of the child's individual characteristics upon the parent (Thomas, Chess, & Birch, 1968).

With the specific application of the general process of interactionism, in the early 1960s I coined the term "goodness of fit" and the related ideas of consonance and dissonance as a useful conceptualization. I proposed this idea to Alex and Herb Birch. They immediately accepted it as a meaningful and significant formulation, and the three of us proceeded to spell out its elaboration.

THE DEFINITIVE FORMULATION OF THE GOODNESS OF FIT CONCEPT

Goodness of fit results when the organism's capacities, motivations, and style of behavior and the environmental demands and expectations are in accord. Such consonance between organism and environment potentiates optimal positive development. Should there be dissonance between the capacities and characteristics of the organism, on the one hand, and the environmental opportunities and demands, on the other hand, there is poorness of fit, which leads to maladaptive functioning and distorted development.

The following two case histories are cited to illustrate the goodness of fit formulation.

CASE HISTORY 1

Gloria had been, from infancy, biologically irregular and had withdrawn from new foods, people, places, and routines. While she eventually adapted to most of these, it was at a very slow pace and took a seemingly endless time. Faced with new stimuli, she expressed her discomfort intensely, and from toddler period on she had frequent tantrums, which often occurred in public places such as supermarkets and street corners—the places where restrictions were necessary for safety or social purposes. So many of these confrontations occurred daily that Gloria was more often in a negative than in a positive mood. When she was 4 years old, her parents needed help. She was a "difficult," "spirited," "challenging" child.

It was interesting and reassuring that Gloria often showed another side in her behavior. Once she had achieved familiarity with people, places, and safety rules, she openly expressed an infectious pleasure. From a temperament point of view, the degree of intensity of her pleasure matched that of her displeasure; there was a world of difference between interacting with a screaming child in the midst of a tantrum and interacting with the same child setting a mood of exuberant joy with her own zestful pleasure.

Although Gloria's parents, Mr. and Mrs. L., had clear ideas about their responsibilities to keep Gloria safe and physically healthy, to teach her social rules at a pace consonant with her developmental ability, and to expose her to a range of experiences, these principles were hard to put into action. As their attitudes and actions were reviewed with one of us in their call for help, it was clear that Gloria's own temperamental individuality had had a marked modifying effect on her parents' actions. In situation after situation, they had begun to inhibit the degree to which they brought her into circumstances requiring new adaptations—even if these promised to be pleasurable in the end. Mrs. L. did her food shopping while Gloria napped. Rarely did the family eat at restaurants with Gloria. Outings were part of the routine because of the two other children, but it was always correctly anticipated that some unpleasantness would spoil the fun. More and more the parents found themselves buying peace with special unmerited rewards, giving in to inappropriate demands, or making convoluted plans such as arranging for Gloria to stay with Grandma while the rest of the family went visiting. Yet somehow Gloria honored safety rules. She did not touch sharp objects, carried her blunt-ended scissors point down, and could be trusted to wait at the end of the block to hold a parent's hand while crossing the street. These had been learned slowly with much protest and even physical struggle, but her parents knew that here there could be no compromise and now these behaviors were routine.

The parental goals were easily categorized: (1) they must end Gloria's reign as family tyrant before she and they were set in this mold; (2) they must prepare her for the educational demands that would begin soon with age 5 and kindergarten; (3) they must stop thinking of Gloria as the family monster and prevent her from becoming just that.

However, there was a distinctly poor fit between Gloria's temperamental individuality and parental handling, and her parents, by themselves, could not achieve these goals. I (S.C.) initiated parent guidance by recommending a series of specific methods for changing their behavior with Gloria.

First, the basic strategy of changing a poorness of fit to a goodness of fit was explained. In the early months, the basic tasks were maintaining nourishment, cleanliness, and health. They accomplished these by simply going with the flow of an irregular child's sleep, hunger, and elimination following the child's temperamental individuality. They learned that a new food would be rejected and spat out, with whining or crying. Her parents then discovered that the same food was accepted with smiles and an open mouth after the sixth presentation spread out over several weeks. Through repetition her parents helped Gloria achieve a good fit. The same pattern occurred when the horror of the struggling infant's first bath turned into a fun time after 3 weeks.

But this positive achievement in infancy became a different story when Gloria reached ages 3 and 4 and more complex positive behavioral patterns were required. The parents were just unable to achieve them as they had been able to with the simple issues in infancy. The bath was a good illustration. To save time, all three children were bathed together. Since Gloria and her two siblings now loved this experience, it was one high point of the day. Yet when they were taken out of the bath, Jane and Larry joined the game of being cuddled in a towel, trying to put on their own pajamas, settling down to story time, but this was not how it went with Gloria. She insisted on staying in the bath and shrieked when her mother finally lifted her out. Both parents would try to explain to Gloria that Jane and Larry both had finished bath time cheerfully, and that she should too. If she kept on screaming she would just spoil the pleasant time for the other two and couldn't go on to story-telling time. When Gloria shrieked "No, no," the parents interpreted this to mean, "You spoiled my bath time, and I don't care if I'm upsetting my sister and brother." Her parents would then explode at Gloria and accuse her of deliberately trying to take all the attention from the other two children. Often all was a shamble—Gloria and the parents would be shrieking and accusing each other of being bad, and by then the other two children would be in tears. Finally, when the combat subsided and the children went to bed, the parents would be exhausted and furious at Gloria.

With the parents' assigning to Gloria a malignant motivation of a highly sophisticated nature improbable in a 4-year-old, the evidence of a poorness of fit was dramatized. Yet, since her parents were genuinely seeking to establish a close and loving relationship with Gloria, it was not difficult to draw parallels between their spontaneous respect for Gloria's temperamental individuality in infancy while seeing to her needs, and achieving the same task with a competent 4-year-old. First it was necessary to retranslate Gloria's screaming, her attempts to prolong the bath, and her declaration "I hate you" into a simple desire—wanting to prolong the bath because she enjoyed it. This desire was being expressed by a child for whom changes and transitions were difficult, who expressed her feelings with high intensity, and who, developmentally and intellectually, could not possibly understand that she was spoiling the pleasure of everyone else.

The first step in their empowerment—in their beginning to achieve a goodness of fit—was for the mother and father to put themselves in Gloria's skin, to empathize with her feelings. Gloria could be left in the bath while the other children were powdered and gotten ready for the night. When Gloria was lifted out of the now dry tub and screaming, wrapped in a towel in a safe place, she would be told that it was story time and that when she finished screaming she could come and listen. No confrontation—in its place a statement that the routine went on and that she was welcome. There would be no punishment for her being her intense self. Any disliked consequence such as missing the story would be a unilateral result of her own actions. Since her parents had not engaged in a battle, when Gloria was ready to join she was able to be welcomed with genuine acceptance. With this regime, just as Gloria had eventually gotten to like a range of foods, she gradually joined in the postbath fun.

After several weeks of this bath routine, the parents were ready to tackle the next seemingly insurmountable problem. Again their perception was that Gloria always wanted it to be her way, this time referring to Gloria's irregular sleep pattern. Her fussing and talking at night disturbed Jane and Larry, who needed their sleep. Nightly threats and scolding had been of no avail. Once again, knowledge of Gloria's pertinent temperament qualities gave her parents empowerment. Gloria wasn't out to "get" her brother and sister nor had she been initially in a power struggle with her parents. She just was not sleepy. Once this was recognized as a long established characteristic, a solution was easy to find: Put Jane and Larry to bed in their parents' room, leaving sleepless Gloria in her own room. The rules were that she must not leave the room or call except for real need, her lights could be on, and she could play quietly alone. There was no battle. After all, if one parent couldn't sleep, reading quietly in another room was no issue. Now Gloria's biologic irregularity was not permitted to create a tyrant, Gloria learned that she must respect her sibs' need for sleep and her parents' need for time for themselves. The power struggles of the poorness of fit era which had been totally unproductive were replaced by goodness of fit routines which restored parental empowerment, regained respect for Gloria's individuality, taught social lessons appropriate to developmental levels, and placed relationships and development on positive terms.

CASE HISTORY 2

I (S.C.) was referred to a mother with a number of complaints about her son. Jamie couldn't get ready for school on time, but he loved to go to school. He was a 9-year-old boy, considered by family, friends, and teachers as a thoughtful child who helped out without being asked, accommodated easily to changes of plans, seemed to fit in equally with new acquaintances or old friends. He was a pleasure to have around. His mother's friends could not understand her constant complaints, although they acknowledged Jamie to be a forgetter. He left his coat on the sofa, couldn't remember where he had put his homework assignment, forgot to take out the garbage, took forever to get to bed. And to cap it all, mornings were a constant commotion. Added to his problem of forgetting was his problem of selecting clothing—one pair of pants was too tight, the other was scratchy, the label of his shirt tickled. Only one outfit passed muster. When Jamie's mother began to say that Jamie was "out to make me miserable," the danger flag went up. Clearly this was an example of a poorness of fit between mother and son. The mother's contention was that since Jamie's younger brother could manage to remember and would wear whatever she laid out for him the night before, Jamie, being older, must be capable of behaving like his brother. And since no one else complained, Jamie's annoying behavior must be aimed at her.

The analysis of Jamie's temperamental qualities was enlightening. His high approach, speedy adaptations, and positive moods did make him welcome most places, but since infancy, the quality of high distractibility had been prominent. This had posed no problems in the early years since he could easily be purposely sidetracked from exploring dangerous or breakables objects. As he grew older, he continued to find stimuli of all kinds attractive. Having high sensitivity (or low threshold), he was the one who saw the daytime moon in the sky, noticed his mother's new hairstyle, comforted other children. But when time was of the essence, these sidetracks on the way to bed (putting a forgotten puzzle away, remembering a message from the teacher) led to his mother's exasperated explosion. His mother, being an individual too, was orderly, time conscious, and intense in expressiveness. Jamie's low threshold also contributed to his intense discomfort with tight bands around his abdomen, stiff fabrics, labels dangling against his back.

This was a situation in which the mother's personal characteristics determined the outcome. The father, who had a private positive relationship with Jamie, had long since retired from the conflict. The mother, it turned out, was also a person of low threshold. She could easily empathize with Jamie's tactile discomforts and found it possible to bring him in on the clothes buying. But in no way could she countenance the idea of distractibility. Jamie, after all, was devastated to miss a planned outing because he had been distracted by an unexpected phone call. But to his mother, his forgetting had to be deliberate, and lateness was an affront designed to make her appear negligent.

Techniques of cooperative functioning that would have worked at school and with friends were discussed with both mother and son. Here we ended with mixed results. One aspect of the morning hassle—the issue of skin discomfort—was changed from a poor fit to a good fit. But distractibility was a lost cause. However, for a 9-year-old boy, life is no longer confined to home. In the world of school and peers, his positive functioning was greatly valued. His distractibility was even a source of amusement. Fortunately, this child achieved a positive sense of personal value and had a basically good fit with the demands of his world.

Goodness of fit and consonance, poorness of fit and dissonance are mere abstractions. They have meaning only in terms of the values and demands of a given socioeconomic group or culture. There is no implication in the concept of goodness of fit that stress and conflict are absent. Quite the contrary is true. Stress and conflict are essential aspects of the developmental process, in which new demands and expectations for enhanced levels of functioning occur continuously, keeping step with the ever-increasing capacities of the growing child. When these enlarging stresses, demands, and conflicts are in harmony with emerging developmental capacities and potentials, then the consequences of such stress are constructive, not harbingers of behavioral disturbance. Rather, it is the excessive stress due to poorness of fit that results in behavior problems.

THE RANGE OF THE APPLICATION OF THE GOODNESS OF FIT

We defined and elaborated the concept of goodness of fit in our exploration toward a comprehensive rational model that would explain the dynamics of the development of a child's healthy or pathological psychological functioning. As we reviewed our clinical experience and various articles in the literature, we reached several conclusions with regard to the application of goodness of fit.

One bright young schoolchild afflicted with severe dyslexia was fortunate that a good teacher quickly recognized the reason for the child's difficulty in learning to read, notified the parents, and arranged for an excellent remedial teacher. Taught in a technique consonant with his perceptive strengths, the child became a good reader and a fine student, and developed an important enhancement of self-esteem at his mastery of a difficult and important task. This sequence was a goodness of fit.

By contrast, a similarly bright child afflicted with severe dyslexia was tragically assigned to a teacher who had not even known the word "dyslexia," and followed the rigid schedule of the fixed curriculum with pupils decade after decade. The teacher became impatient at the child's stumbling efforts to read and scolded the youngster for being "lazy" and "disobedient." Taking up the teacher's cue, the child became the class scapegoat. The teacher gave a highly unfavorable report of the child at the parent–teacher conference. The parents, who had no understanding of dyslexia, could only accept the teacher's verdict. They were shocked, received no useful advice, and were only told to enforce the child's disorganized homework efforts. The outcome was sadly predictable. The child learned only slowly and over the years hated school more and more. Since school forms a significant portion of a child's task and social existence and since there was no counteractive support from family, the barrages of criticism and teasing by adults and peers resulted in the child developing pathogenic self-defeating defensive mechanisms in a failed effort to hide deficiencies. This story was indeed a poorness of fit based, not on temperament, but on an unrecognized and unrespected variant developmental pattern.

These stories of the two children with dyslexia, one with goodness of fit, the other with poorness of fit, can be duplicated with one or another variation with children with any special characteristics—a deep interest in and commitment to music that is demeaned, a subtle physical handicap interfering with athletics, mild recognized or unrecognized neonatal brain damage, and so forth.

The concept of goodness of fit has also been applied by the eminent biologist René Dubos to physical health. "Health can be regarded as an expression of fitness to the environment, as a state of adaptedness. . . . The words health and disease are meaningful only when defined in terms of a given person's functioning in a given physical and social environment" (Dubos, 1965, pp. 350–351). The concept of goodness of fit is similar to that employed by the developmental psychologist Jerome Kagan (1971) in his study of perceptual schemata in infants and their interaction with new environmental stimuli. He emphasized that excessive stress and distress will depend on a discrepancy from an established schema that the infant cannot assimilate, and not on the novelty or change in stimulation as such. On the cognitive level, Hunt (1980) had emphasized what he calls "the problem of the match" between children's cognitive capacity and the demands made on them. If a demand is dissonant with their cognitive level, children show "withdrawal and distress, and often tears;" if consonant, the task is performed with "interest and joyful excitement" (Hunt, 1980, pp. 34–35).

These early formulations of a related concept of goodness of fit were of interest in specific interactional individual-environment situations, but were limited in the application of broader significance.

By contrast, the concept of goodness of fit has led us to the development of prevention, early intervention, and treatment methods for children with problems through the process of parent guidance.

9

PARENT GUIDANCE

Parent guidance, based on the concept of goodness of fit, represents a most valuable treatment strategy in child psychiatry. By this procedure, we mean the formulation of a program of altered functioning by the parents that could ameliorate excessive and harmful stress for the child. Whenever indicated, guidance of the parents can also include recommendations for other appropriate environmental changes that the parents can implement, such as a change in school placement or alteration of living arrangements for the child (Thomas et al., 1968, pp. 171–181).

The basic emphasis in parent guidance is on the change in the parents' *behavior* and *overtly expressed attitudes,* and not on the definition or changes of underlying conflicts, anxieties, or defenses in the parent. The goal of parent guidance, in other words, is to change specific aspects of the parents' actual functioning with their child, but not to delineate or attempt to change directly any of their covert attitudes or defense mechanisms that presumably might be related to overt behavior and attitudes.

Such an approach assumes that a child's behavior problem does not necessarily reflect the existence of deep-seated anxieties, conflicts, or maladaptive conditioned reflex patterns that must be eliminated for treatment to be successful. Parent guidance may even be effective in ameliorating or resolving some of the parents' deep-seated anxieties and conflicts, either by itself or in combination with direct treatment of the child. When it comes to serious psychopathology in the child, such as autism, childhood schizophrenia, or organic brain syndromes, the therapeutic role of parent guidance may be more modest.

Parent guidance procedures also assume that parental functioning that is detrimental to a child's psychological development does not necessarily reflect the presence of deep-seated anxieties, conflicts, or pathological goals in the parents that must be changed before the child's symptoms can be ameliorated. It also assumes that if one or both parents do have some significant degree of psychopathology, this does not necessarily prevent them from making the changes in the specific behaviors that are proving detrimental to the child's psychological welfare. Anna Freud has put it well. She "refuse[s] to believe that mothers need to change their personalities before they can change the handling of their child" (Freud, 1960, p. 37).

CASE ILLUSTRATION

Our experience is in agreement with Anna Freud's contention. In one especially interesting example of such maternal change in behavior, the combination of maternal determination and the child's temperamental characteristics were essential in the transformation of a poor fit into a goodness of fit.

A mother and a child were referred to me (S.C.) by the director of a nursery school. The story was that Tom's mother, Mrs. S., had remained in the classroom for the first 3 weeks after admission because of Tom's crying and clinging when she tried to leave. The school policy was to permit this briefly. All the other mothers had at most remained for a week while their children settled in. The director observed that Tom made friends and essentially ignored his mother's presence. When his mother finally left, Tom cried loudly but almost immediately after her disappearance he stopped crying and seemed happy. Mrs. S., who had in fact lingered in the office ready to return to the classroom, was thunderstruck when Tom stopped crying and didn't need her perpetual reassurance to comfort him. Mrs. S. was then convinced that her behavior was inhibiting Tom's development and dooming him to become an anxious child. She asked the school director for help for herself, and he referred her to me.

In my consultation it emerged that Mrs. S. did have a classical anxiety neurosis. She was claustrophobic and had panic attacks. She had started psychoanalysis but could not tolerate the introspection. She entreated me to help and promised to follow all instructions. In my play diagnostic observation of Tom, with his mother in an adjoining room, Tom soon ignored her and settled in to play happily and interdependently with me. Developmentally, he was a competent and verbal 3-year-old, with no unusual feature. Temperamentally, he was an adaptable, approachable child with positive mood and moderate intensity.

In essence, my treatment strategy was aimed at freeing Tom of responsibility for his mother's vulnerable psychological state by conditioning Mrs. S. in small increments. Tom liked to visit other children and did so with ease if he went directly to the other child's home on the same school bus. But if he went home first and was taken by his mother, he would implore her to stay—which she did. When visits directly from school became frequent, Mrs. S. began to have anxiety attacks in the middle of the visit and would phone to reassure herself of Tom's contentment. As Tom heard the other mother assuring his mother, he would become upset, take the phone crying and beg his mother to be taken home. The solution required two goals: Tom's independence and his mother's reassurance. I advised Mrs. S. that when she phoned she should use a cheerful voice. If during the few moments of chatting with the other mother, she would hear Tom playing contentedly, then, she should recognize that his obligatory crying was only a token gesture. This strategy had a remarkably reassuring effect on Mrs. S. When she was separated from Tom her anxiety diminished.

The final scenario was quite dramatic. Having watched his classmates get off the bus and walk by themselves into their apartment buildings without a waiting parent, Tom demanded of his mother that he be permitted to do the same. The big day came. Tom got off the bus, waved triumphantly to the children, turned, and saw his mother just then returning from food shopping—her maneuver impelled by her anxiety. Seeing his mother "waiting," Tom had a mammoth tantrum, an action quite out of character. He was devastated, his mother was shocked, and the importance of his need to be free of her anxiety had been made clear. I suggested that, since the apartment was at the front of the house, she position herself at a window but hidden from view. Thus she could monitor Tom's safety while lessening her anxiety and, at the same time, allow him to retain his 3-year-old dignity. The success of this plan turned out to serve as a further reassurance. She was now certain that Tom would no longer accept peaceably the role of troubled child she had assigned him and would express his clear and strong demand for his independence. She learned that ways could be devised to assuage her own anxiety without a pernicious effect on his development. Mrs. S. remained a prisoner of her own psychiatric problems but was happier knowing that Tom's welfare would not be affected.

Parent guidance has the great virtue of enlisting the parents as direct allies in the therapeutic process, allies whose influence on the child is continuous and intimate from day to day. It is the very rare parent who does not really wish the child a healthy, happy, and productive future, no matter whether the parent's behavior is serving to promote or undermine this goal. It is the consonance of mental health professionals and parents in their concern for the child's welfare that makes this therapeutic alliance possible. Parent guidance also involves advice couched in practical terms and spelled out with regard to the specific items of the behavior to be changed. As such, the guidance recommendations are easily understood and make no demands that are beyond the capacities of the average parent. When effective, this approach avoids the necessity for long and expensive direct treatment of the child. In some cases, where direct psychotherapy of the child is required, simultaneous parent guidance may expedite significantly the course of the child's treatment. And finally, when effective, parent guidance also bypasses the alternative approach of an analysis of the parent's own psychopathological patterns, a procedure that is likely to be prolonged, arduous, and expensive.

APPLICATION OF PARENT GUIDANCE

Once the clinical evaluation of a child has been completed, and a diagnosis of a behavior disorder made, an analysis of the NYLS and clinical data identifies the specific features of child and environment that, in interaction with each other, are producing the poorness of fit and consequent psychopathological development. Once these specific features are identified, a program can then be formulated that will relieve the excessive stress the child is experiencing and ameliorate the symptoms of the behavior disorder.

On the basis of this analysis, parent guidance was offered to each set of parents. In almost all cases, the parents gladly accepted this offer. In one case, the severity of the child's symptoms in school and with peers was such that psychotherapy was recommended concurrently with parent guidance. In another case, the parents decided to arrange for psychotherapy on their own, despite the recommendation that they first try the guidance procedure.

This strategy of parent guidance rests on the commitment to an *individualization* of the treatment strategy for any child and set of parents. With this commitment, counseling in general global terms is considered inadequate and even counterproductive. What is necessary, rather, is the identification of the specifics of the poorness of fit in each individual case, and this may vary qualitatively from one child to another.

The initial parent guidance session in each case started with our affirmation of the parents' concern for their child's welfare and joint interest in eliminating the symptoms that were jeopardizing the youngster's happiness and functioning. We urged both parents to participate in the guidance discussions, and in most cases this was achieved. With both parents present, if conflict and disagreement between them became evident, it could be emphasized that they were still committed to their child's interests and needs.

The rationale of the guidance program was then explained to the parents in terms of the concept of a goodness of fit between the child's characteristics and the parents' functioning as the essential basis for the youngster's healthy psychological development. The specific area or areas in which a poorness rather than a goodness of fit existed were then identified. This involved a description of the child's temperament, of any other child attributes that were pertinent, and of the particular parental behaviors and attitudes that, in interaction with the child's characteristics, were producing excessive stress. Other relevant factors where they existed, such as inappropriate school expectations, were also defined.

Throughout this discussion the parents were assured that the poorness of fit formulation in no way meant they were "bad parents," and that the same behavior on their part with a child with different attributes might have been positive rather than negative in its consequences. It was also emphasized that the child's disturbed responses to their well-meaning efforts did not mean that the youngster was "sick," "bad," or "willfully disobedient." This focus helped to clarify the basic thesis that the necessity for parental change in attitudes and behavior did not mean that they had wanted to harm the child. It was a question of lack of knowledge, misinformation, and confusion, rather than motivation, that had led to undesirable consequences for the child.

The parents were then offered specific suggestions and advice for changing their identified harmful attitudes and practices. Reference to concrete incidents in the child's life were made to illustrate each recommendation. For example, the initial intense negative responses to new situations and slow adaptability of a temperamentally difficult child were documented by details of the child's history with new foods, new people, new activities, new school situations, and so on. These reactions were distinguished from anxiety or motivated negativism. The recommendations for parental change then followed logically, in terms of the goal of quiet, firm, and consistent handling, with patient expectation that positive adaptation would occur after a number of exposures to the particular new demand. It was also emphasized that whenever possible the youngster should be exposed to only one or two new situations at a time, so as not to overwhelm the child's capacity for adaptation. At the same time, shielding the child from *any* new demands and experiences to avoid the turmoil and tension these produced in child, parent, and bystander was highly undesirable, for it left the youngster overprotected and unable to transform new stressful settings into habitual positive ones. A healthy self-esteem also could not develop without repeated experiences of successful mastery of the new.

The guidance formulation for the slow-to-warm-up child was essentially similar to that for the difficult child. Here, it was usually easier for the parents to carry through a quiet, patient regime, inasmuch as the youngster's withdrawal from the new did not produce the noisy embarrassing turmoil characteristic of the difficult child's response pattern to the new. As another example, the restlessness and shifts in attention of a high active and

distractible youngster were distinguished from "lazi-
ness," willful inattention, and lack of interest. The necessity for giving such a child periodic breaks, whether on
long automobile trips or while doing homework, was
spelled out in detail.

In most cases of behavior disorder in early and middle
childhood, poorness of fit involved some feature of the
child's temperamental characteristics as a major issue.
Other factors did play a significant role in certain cases,
such as a parent's difficulty in accepting a child's intellectual limitations or in understanding the organic basis of
a dyslexic syndrome. Whatever the issue, the basic strategy of parent guidance was similar. The cornerstone was
always the delineation of the *specific* nature of the pathogenic child–environment interactional process in each *individual* case, and the tailoring of a guidance program
concretely to that *individual* situation.

An essential feature of the guidance program was a systematic follow-up schedule with the parents after the initial session. Even with parents who were eager and able
to carry through the schedule of behavioral change recommendations, more than one discussion was usually necessary for them to be implemented fully. Several sessions
were usually required for the parents to be able to grasp
adequately the concept of the child's individuality and
its influence on the youngster's ability to cope with parental and other environmental demands and expectations.
At these follow-up discussions, the parents' behavior in
a number of specific incidents that had occurred in the
interim period was reviewed. This review, done in detail,
was usually required to aid the parents in becoming adept
at identifying those situations in the child's daily life in
which modification of their techniques of management
was needed.

Inevitably, the guidance sessions revealed defensiveness, anxiety, or guilt in a number of parents, in addition to misconceptions, misinformation, and confusion.
It was often possible, in the course of clarifying the dy-

namics of the behavior problem development and of
pointing the way for the parents to actively resolve their
child's problem, to relieve effectively these disturbed parental cognitive and affective reactions. In other cases,
these parental attitudes reflected significant psychopathology that was not amenable to the therapeutic strategy
of parent guidance. The same was true of the instances in
which other types of symptomatic expression of parental
psychopathology, such as neurotic needs for domination,
or intrusive or passive submissiveness, served as an important and even decisive influence on the child's behavior disorder development.

PARENT GUIDANCE SUCCESSES

Parent guidance was evaluated by qualitative clinical
judgment as moderately or highly successful in approximately 67% of the 42 NYLS childhood behavior disorder
cases. This rating was estimated both by the indication of
parental change in the desired direction and by improvement in the behavior disorder, two factors that went hand
in hand in a reciprocal relationship. When the initial efforts of change by the parents brought quick positive
change in the child's functioning, this acted as a powerful
stimulus for the parents to continue and extend their altered behavior and attitudes. An average of only two to
three guidance sessions was required for this successful
outcome.

A positive parental response to the guidance approach
was found with children with all types of temperamental
patterns, except for those with high distractibility and
low persistence. (The reasons for this unfavorable response in this latter group will be addressed in the next
section.) In the successful cases, the parents were able to
understand and accept the judgment that their child's disturbed behavior did not reflect any deep-seated psychopathology and that the need for change on their part did not

indict them as "bad parents." Furthermore, the validity of their goals and aspirations for the child's future was affirmed. With these assurances, they were able to accept and implement the need for a modification in their approach to the child if their goals were to be achieved.

PARENT GUIDANCE FAILURES

In the other 33% of cases, however, parent guidance was unsuccessful, as judged by the lack of any significant change in the behavior and attitudes that had entered into the formation of a poorness of fit and behavior disorder development. In some cases, only one or two guidance discussions were attempted, because of the parent's fixed refusal to consider that his or her functioning was undesirable. In other instances, lip service was given to the recommendations for change, or apparently earnest efforts were made to follow the outlined program, but a number of discussions then revealed that nothing had changed. And in a few cases, a parent was willing to come for a number of guidance sessions but made it clear that this was not acceptance of our judgments and suggestions. One father even put it that "I know exactly what you're going to say," then proceeded to give a caricature of the discussion in the previous sessions and continued to go his own way.

The reasons for the failure of parent guidance were varied. One striking finding was the uniform failure in the four children who were temperamentally highly distractible and nonpersistent. It was clear in each case that the parents could not accept these characteristics as normal. These middle- and upper-middle-class parents attached great importance to educational achievement for both their daughters and their sons, and to success in professional careers or business for the boys. For both of these goals, persistence and low distractibility, that is, "stick-to-itiveness," were considered laudable and even essential. It was, therefore, difficult for these parents to accept the characteristics at the other extreme, nonpersistence and high distractibility, especially in boys. In this regard, it is of interest that these four cases were all boys. In a few cases, this attitude was expressed openly in the guidance sessions, with such remarks about the child as, "He lacks character." We might speculate that with parents espousing different sociocultural values, parent guidance for distractible children might be more successful.

In several other cases, rigid parental standards that led to excessive demands on the child could not be influenced in the guidance sessions. Parental denial of their child's limitations also proved inflexible to change in several cases. The parents who failed to carry out the guidance recommendations were not prepared to face the implication that this might be due to their own psychological problems. Either they gave lip service to the endeavor, reporting that they were carrying through the necessary changes when it was clear that this was not the case, or they "misinterpreted" our suggestions, or they minimized the problem, or they simply politely but firmly disagreed with us. They were quite willing to consider that the child might need direct psychotherapy and to make the necessary arrangements, but not that they themselves might require treatment. At least several of these parents had had extensive courses of psychotherapy in their earlier years, which they referred to openly, but this also did not facilitate any self-scrutiny in the guidance sessions. To have pressed the issue of their own problems, which we tried tentatively on some occasions, would only have alienated them, with loss of whatever influence, no matter how little, we still had on the child's developmental course.

PARENT GUIDANCE IN ADOLESCENCE

For teenagers, it was the demands of their peer groups and their schools that were typically most influential in shaping either healthy or pathological adaptations. In some cases, a deviant developmental course had had its onset in childhood with a pathogenic parent–child interaction, and it was not until adolescence that the consequences became evident in the crystallization of a behavior disorder. However, in these instances, the symptoms also reflected the youngster's difficulties outside the home more than any continuing problem of relationships with the parents.

As a result, the influence of parents, for good or bad, was no longer the preeminent environmental factor that it had been in the childhood years. With teenagers, parent guidance, even when the parents cooperated fully, did not have the same dramatic effect by itself as it did in the successful cases in childhood. Guidance was useful, and in some cases very valuable, but direct treatment of the teenager was usually also essential. One girl, Lily, was an exception. Her family had moved frequently because of her father's work assignments, and she lacked the environmental stability and continuity to ameliorate her difficulties with impulse control. She became involved in a number of thoughtless but not serious delinquent acts. The parents were advised to set firm rules quietly and to stabilize the living situation for their daughter. This they did and Lily recovered quickly. In several cases the parents arranged for treatment of their teenager on their own without consulting us, so that an attempt at parent guidance was not possible.

The number of adolescent cases with parent guidance is too small to permit any definitive conclusions, but it is our impression that a greater percentage of the parents were less responsive than were those in the childhood behavior disorder series. Most likely, this reflected the thrust of our judgments that change on their part might be helpful, but would not by itself produce a dramatic improvement in their troubled teenager. However, in those cases where the parents were responsible, the guidance discussions were helpful and well worth the effort.

PARENT GUIDANCE IN CLINICAL PRACTICE

In a child psychiatric practice extending over many years, I (S.C.) have found the therapeutic procedure of parent guidance to be as valuable as it was with the NYLS families. The clinical approach has been the same, with a delineation in each case of the specific dynamics of the poorness of fit between child and environment responsible for the development of the behavior problem for which the parents sought professional help. Based on this analysis, a program of altered parental functioning supplemented when necessary by remedial tutoring or other special therapeutic procedures was recommended to the parents, in the same manner as outlined earlier with the NYLS families.

The majority of parents accepted the logic of the guidance recommendations, appeared pleased to assume the role of therapeutic allies, and attempted seriously to carry through the necessary changes in their own functioning. In some cases, only a few discussions were necessary for the parents to modify their approach to the child and for the positive effect of this change on the child's behavior to become evident. No systematic follow-up of this clinical series has been possible. In a number of cases, informal follow-up revealed a continued benign and healthy developmental course on the child's part. In other instances, the parents returned, months or even several years later, because of a recurrence of the child's difficulties. In most of these cases, it was evident that the parents had not sustained the necessary change in their functioning, and this was then corrected by a review of the issues as originally defined. In a smaller number of cases, the analysis of the reasons for the recurrences of old symptoms or the appearance of new ones in the child revealed evidence of more severe psychopathology than originally estimated, or of special problems on the parents' part in implementing the guidance program. Either direct treatment of the child or more extensive guidance sessions with the parents, or both, were then necessary.

In some cases, a positive parental response to the guidance program was not sufficient by itself to resolve the child's behavior problem. This occurred typically when the disturbed behavior had been present for several years or more, resulting in one or another fixed, self-defeating defensive pattern. In such cases, direct treatment of the child was necessary, supplemented by a prolonged series of parent guidance discussions.

In a minority of instances in which parents came for consultative evaluation of their child's problems, they refused categorically to participate in the guidance program. It was evident that they expected the psychiatrist to take over the burden of caring for their child. Rather than being willing to assume an active role in their child's treatment as the psychiatrist's allies, they expected to be relieved of all such responsibility. These parents did not return after the nature of the guidance program had been explained, and undoubtedly went "shopping" until they found a professional approach to their liking.

OVERVIEW

The therapeutic strategy of parent guidance, as we have formulated it, has proved an effective treatment modality in perhaps 50% of children with behavior disorders. If the diagnosis was made quickly after the onset of the disorder, then the guidance program in the successful cases usually required only a few discussions. If the condition had been chronic before treatment was started, with fixed defensive reaction patterns already established in the child, then direct treatment of the child was often required, in addition to a prolonged series of guidance sessions. This experience argues strongly for the value of early diagnosis and treatment of behavior disorders in children.

The usefulness of this parent guidance approach indicates the practical value of the goodness-of-fit model. With this conceptual framework, it has been possible to individualize the treatment approach to fit the needs of each child and to identify concretely the behavioral and attitudinal changes on the parents' part required to change a pathogenic interaction with the child into a healthy relationship.

Part II

New Applications to the Theory and Practice of Temperament

10

THE RAPID EXPANSION OF TEMPERAMENT PRACTICE AND THEORY SINCE 1970

The previous chapters have detailed our methods and findings of the basic definition, categorization, and ratings of temperament. These studies led us to the analysis of the individual–environmental interactional process and then to the concept of goodness of fit. This formulation led to a systematic parent guidance process in applying prevention, early intervention, and effective therapy to children with behavior disorders.

Our early publications of the late 1950s and the 1960s attracted the reports and ideas of a relatively small number of influential students of behavior, including the child psychiatrists Leon Eisenberg, Michael Rutter, and John Rose; the pediatricians Barry Brazelton and William Carey; and the developmental psychologists Arthur Jersild and Jerome Kagan. Their interest and encouragement were of great support to us in those early days when we began to challenge so many entrenched theoretical and clinical positions.

Through the 1960s, the influence of this group, supplemented by our regular professional publications and lectures, resulted in a slow but consistent increase in the acceptance of the importance of temperament by researchers and clinicians in the mental health profession and education.

As philosophers have pointed out, with change, quantity traditionally becomes transformed into quality. We can place the watershed to the early 1970s as the time when our concepts and practical formulations entered the mainstream of normal and deviant psychological theory and practice.

Since the 1970s a stream, even a flood, of talented students and workers have explored and pursued the many implications of the significance of temperament:

- A temperamental component has been elaborated in parent guidance provided by professional and community health care and child-care units.
- The application of temperament within pediatric and nursing care, within the school setting, and to the handicapped child has become more frequent.
- There has been a solid flow of investigations into the biological basis of temperament, cultural factors, and the ramifications of expanded and modified concepts of temperament and goodness of fit.
- Finally, but not least, the application of temperament has necessitated an examination of the need for revision of traditional and limited methods of clinical practice.

By the 1990s the significance of temperament had flowered and was accepted in the professional fields to the extent that Leon Eisenberg commented that our "insights have been so thoroughly incorporated into the mainstream of theory and clinical practice in psychiatry and pediatrics that it may be difficult for students to recognize how revolutionary they were 36 years ago" (Eisenberg, 1994, p. 285).

In the following chapters we will review the specific areas enumerated above. In the growing and maturing field of temperament, many modifications, criticisms, and even variations in our basic formulations have arisen. These critiques and suggested changes deserve serious consideration and respect.

11

PARENT AND CHILD EDUCATION ABOUT TEMPERAMENT

Sandra was born of an easy pregnancy and delivery into a stable and healthy family. But, as early as in her second month, it was clear that her care was not easy, whether with sleeping or feeding schedules, her mood, or the speed of her adaptation to any change. Her father, an eminent research and developmental psychologist, was well versed with the phenomena of temperament. He quickly recognized that Sandra's behavior showed the typical normal pattern of difficult temperament.

With that recognition, both parents knew how to properly handle Sandra's irregular sleeping and feeding schedule, her shrieks with her first baths, her spitting out violently a new food, and so on. She was a demanding child, but with her parents' patient and clear responses, Sandra gradually adapted her life routines as she grew older. Her parents were rewarded by her delightful and spirited expressiveness whenever her positive intense temperament reactions responded to her adjusted situations.

When she was enrolled in nursery school she reacted with turmoil, as her parents expected. But since they knew what to expect and do, and had coached the teacher, Sandra adjusted within a few weeks and sailed through a relaxed, happy nursery school experience. Yet when she moved to first grade at a new school, the story was not so simple. She was faced with a new school room, and a strange teacher and classmates. She was also faced with having to learn in a formal manner, very different from just playing in nursery school, and with all kinds of new expectations and demands on her behavior. She exploded into a real wingding tantrum, and refused to go to school the next morning. Both parents insisted that she had to go, no matter how unpleasant it was, that her adjustment to school was crucial. Sandra knew that her parents were flexible and permissive with many situations, but at certain times they would be adamant, and this was one. So Sandra went to school, had a miserable time, and was unhappy at home the rest of the day. The rest of the story was predictable. Sandra's distress subsided week by week, and after a month she had adapted and began to enjoy school.

With the demands of her new school now familiar, she went through the following years in a breeze. She had good intelligence, learning was a pleasure, and she was an excellent student. Also, once she adapted, she easily made friends who enjoyed her positive, spirited temperament.

As she went through her elementary years, Sandra was a delightful youngster for her parents, brothers, and relatives—bright, curious about learning, cheerfully cooperative about the household chores, and busy with her interests and social life. There were scarcely any problems until she was 12 and scheduled to change to junior high school.

Suddenly, one day, Sandra came home tearful, and when her parents came in, she exploded, sobbing, "I was just told today at school that next year I will have to go to this new junior high school. I got very upset, I can't go to that new school. I'm scared. What can I do?" The parents were unhappy at her acute distress, but not shocked or demoralized. They knew what had happened. They sat down in her bedroom, comforted her, and waited for a half-hour until she stopped crying and looking bewildered. Her father started, with her mother chiming in, "Sandra, we're sorry you are upset. But the answer is clear. Do you remember when you started first grade, how upset you were, and it took you a month to get adjusted? Since then you have been happy in school all these years." Sandra listened, "I do remember, but what has that to do with what's happened to me today?" The father, an excellent teacher, quietly and slowly explained the concept that children have individual differences in their behavior, called temperament. Her temperament was the kind that makes it hard to adjust immediately to something that is different. That's what happened when she started school in first grade, that's why she was upset at having to go to a new and very different school now. And she would get over that, the same as with first grade, but gradually, not all at once.

Sandra listened, still teary, "Maybe, it makes sense, but it's too much for me to really understand. Does it mean I'm not normal?" Her mother soothed, "It is hard to understand something new when you are upset. You are perfectly normal. We have a good book in our library to explain about temperament for parents. Don't try to read it tonight. We will have dinner, then spend the evening listening to your favorite records, and you will get to sleep. Stay home tomorrow, and your father and I will talk with you.'

The next morning the parents sat at their breakfast table, crossing their fingers until Sandra came in. In a few minutes she ran in clutching her book, saying, "Hello, good morning. I woke up early, started reading the book you gave me. Within a few pages I was fascinated, and I just had to read until I just finished it. I am so excited, the book is just about me, now I know what temperament is about." She turned to her father, "You haven't finished your breakfast, but I just have to ask you to explain what you tried to explain to me last night." He nodded, "Just go ahead."

SANDRA: From the book, do I have the temperament called "difficult and spirited"?

FATHER: Yes, indeed, you have had that temperament since you were a baby.

SANDRA: How many children have my kind of temperament?

FATHER: It varies, but it is about 10 or 15 out of 100.

SANDRA: Just my bad luck, to have this problem and most children don't.

FATHER: Sandra, just stop that. Your temperament is perfectly normal. And any temperament has some good qualities and others not so good at some times. When you get frustrated you can get very angry. When you have to adjust to a big new change, like going to the new school, you feel very upset, as you felt yesterday. But there are very good parts of your temperament. When something enjoyable or interesting happens, you feel happy, excited, and jump into the activity with real zest. Those times, and there are many, you become spirited. Also, you will never be a pushover. If someone tries to make you agree right away, like a friend or a group, and if it doesn't make sense, you will say no.

SANDRA: Will I ever change my temperament?

FATHER: That is a basic question that the researchers are trying to answer. But, even if your temperament may not change, you can learn to control your difficulty in adjusting to change.Already you have learned a great deal. You used to have real tantrums when you were frustrated. Whenever you wanted something foolish or too expensive and your mother said no, you would yell and your mother would pull you out of the store, and tell you just to scream as long as you wanted to but that you wouldn't get the item you wanted. When you calmed down, you and she would continue shopping cheerfully together. After a few of those tantrums you learned that your mother wouldn't give in, and you gave them up.

SANDRA: Wow! If my mother gave in I would have become a spoiled brat.

FATHER: Very true. You're a fine girl, we are good friends. We were determined that you would grow up as a delightful person, no matter what your temperament would be.

SANDRA: What should I do to stop me from getting upset?

FATHER: I have a good suggestion. When you are upset at something new, say to yourself, "It's the first grade again." That will remind you that you will be distressed at first but if you stick to it, as we made you do in the first grade, after a short time you will relax and begin to enjoy the new experience. Now that you are growing up, you can do it yourself; we don't have to force you. You can just stick it out like you did in the first grade. And you can use the same rule whenever you get upset at something new and different.

Sandra thanked her parents, ate breakfast, and announced she was going to school. Sandra felt unhappy for about a week, then began to smile and told her parents, "I remember what you told me, I say "It's the first grade again" to myself many times a day, until I feel fine and begin to look forward to the interesting new experiences that I will have when I start junior high school."

LESSONS TO LEARN FROM SANDRA
AND HER PARENTS

In Chapter 9, "Parent Guidance," we focused on spelling out the issues of a poorness of fit between parent and child due to temperament, unhealthy interaction, and its development into the child's behavioral disturbance. From that, we outlined the strategy of counseling the parents for modifying or changing their attitudes to achieve a goodness of fit from a poorness of fit.

Now, in this chapter, with Sandra's story, we raise the importance of parents learning their children's temperaments, and teaching the normal youngsters to understand their own temperaments. Parents can achieve these goals. They don't have to be expert mental professionals, like Sandra's parents.

In the following chapter, "Prevention and Early Intervention in Temperament Programs," we detail the extensive parental education on temperament that is provided in the books and lectures by Mary Kurcinka and Stanley Turecki. Every generation looks for parental child-rearing advice found in a host of books, popular magazines, and newspaper articles. Since the 1970s, the issue of temperament has increasingly been included in these publications one way or another by the writers. For example, Dr. Marc Weissbluth (1987), the Director of the Sleep Disorders Center of Children's Memorial Hospital in Chicago, has published an excellent, practical manual for advising parents on helping their children to sleep well, and includes a discussion of the significance of the influence of the child's temperament. Each year, we get many calls from freelance writers asking for an interview, explaining that they are planning to write a book or magazine article that includes the subject of temperament. Friends and relatives keep telling us, in one incident or another, how they have learned about temperament from their family's pediatrician, or from the instructor in a class on pregnancy and delivery. These days it is not difficult for a parent to learn about temperament; rather, it is difficult to avoid reading or hearing about temperament.

THE IMPORTANCE OF LEARNING ONE'S TEMPERAMENT

The experience of Sandra, cited earlier, is an example of how controlling one's temperament can give that person the confidence to master any special demand or crisis. For so many youngsters or adults, this self-awareness of temperament and how to use it positively can become an important asset for expanding self-confidence and self-esteem.

One young adult who worked on one of our research projects had a slow-to-warm-up temperament. She was assigned to do a new kind of interview with a new teacher in a new school. She was anticipating an uneasy feeling, but had learned how to handle her own temperament, and simply said, "Of course I'm going, I'm shy but I'm not timid." And she did her assignment splendidly.

Unfortunately and inevitably, some parents hear about temperament and misinterpret and misuse this knowledge. One mother's 4-year-old daughter had moderate negative reactions when frustrated. Whenever the child fussed and cried, at any denial of her wishes, even with a trivial issue, the mother gave in and appeased her. The girl was pleased, but was well on the way to becoming a tyrant, dominating her mother. The father objected to his wife's handling of the daughter. But the mother proclaimed, "The girl's temperament will make her a frustrated child with any denial, and it is bad for such a child to be frustrated." Whatever this mother had read or heard about temperament had been upended. She had "learned" the exact opposite caretaking approach to that appropriate for her child's temperament. In school, none of this behavior was reported. If the mother could alter her approach properly, this kind of simple poorness of fit could be corrected, the child's tyranny might vanish, and the child might move on to a healthy development.

12

PREVENTION AND EARLY INTERVENTION IN TEMPERAMENT PROGRAMS

The analysis of the origins and evolution of the behavioral problems in the NYLS led to the formulation of the pathogenesis in each case. The cause of the excessive stress leading to a disorder was defined in most cases in terms of the poorness of fit, that is, dissonance between parental or other environmental demands or expectations and the child's inability to master specific temperamental characteristics or other capacities.

TEMPERAMENT PROGRAMS

Our findings that the pathogenesis of most of the behavioral problems of the NYLS could be attributed to a maladapative parent–child or other interactional process, a poorness of fit, led us to a preventative and therapeutic remediation of the behavior problems through the procedure of parent guidance (see details in Chapter 9).

Our favorable reports of the usefulness of parent guidance (Chapter 9) have encouraged a number of mental health professionals to initiate and expand this therapeutic procedure, which is of special importance in the development of parent guidance programs in health service centers and community programs throughout the United States and Canada.

Some parenting centers had been established before the recognition of the significance of temperament. Those who have been impressed by the importance of temperamental individuality and the concept of goodness of fit for parent guidance have modified or expanded their parent centers to include these temperamental issues.

THE EXPANSION OF TEMPERAMENT PROGRAMS

In recent years, during various professional meetings, invitational lectures and visits to centers, and by many personal communications, we have been struck by the number of temperament programs initiated or expanded year by year. The content of the programs is varied: some elaborate, some simple, some with special innovative ideas, some linked with larger organizational structures. None are stereotyped, but all are focused on the premise of a temperament program that includes prevention of and early intervention with behavior problems in children.

We will describe four temperament programs that are varied in geographic location, size, socioeconomic status of the families, and strategy of the programs. They are summarized below as examples of the type of programs that have been developing. We have visited these programs and found the enthusiastic staffs in all of them to be knowledgeable and committed.

La Grande, Oregon Program

La Grande is located in rural eastern Oregon, the central town of the county. The town population is about 18,500 of a total county population of 22,000. The county's economy is derived mostly from the timber industry and agriculture, and the state college is located in La Grande.

In the 1980s the town had established a general parent guidance center, called the Center for Human Development. One of the center's social workers, Mark Levno, attended a workshop on temperament that we gave in Portland. Levno was excited by the idea that the addition of a temperament program would be an enormous opportunity for the prevention of behavior disorders in children. Levno worked on a draft for a grant for the temperament program from one of the state of Oregon's human services. We assisted by making several suggestions for the proposal. He submitted it to the state in 1988, and it was approved. By then Levno had left for another position, and Bill Smith, an excellent trained psychologist, was appointed director of the program, and immediately plunged into organization, recruitment, and treatment at the temperament center.

The temperament program was established with referrals of families though a wide community outreach—by offering a free "Child Behavior Screening" in Headstart programs, churches, schools, and other groups. By 1994 almost four hundred families were enrolled. A majority of the families were farmers, skilled, or semiskilled workers, with some in lower-middle-class occupations and a few professionals. Fifty percent had an annual income under twenty thousand dollars a year.

The program was based on our theory and practice formulation and structured with sequential phases of intervention, assessment, and specific parenting advice and support. Of special interest was that the program's services were provided by specially trained parents, called temperament specialists, who were supervised by a mental health professional. When screening of these children revealed nontemperamental psychiatric problems, they were referred to a panel of psychiatrists. Seventy-four percent of the families completed the program. In a follow-up with a subjective questionnaire survey, 79% of those parents indicated that they were helped by the program. Objective evidence of the validity of the follow-up was shown when the state legislature threatened to terminate the program. A large number of parents rallied, went to the legislature, lobbied intensively to continue the program, and succeeded (Smith, 1994). Senior staff members have assembled a substantial manual of over three hundred pages that contains the detailed methods, forms, and schedules used in their program, and hope to publish it as a model for temperament parent programs (D. Warsaw, personal communication, 1995).

The program of La Grande has been described in some detail because it has served as an innovative and successful program for unsophisticated parents in a semirural and rather isolated community.

Turecki's New York Program

Dr. Stanley Turecki, trained in child and adult psychiatry and also in psychoanalysis, started in private practice in the early 1970s. He also joined the voluntary part-time staff of the psychiatric department of Beth Israel, a first-class New York hospital. His third child, Jillian, was born normally, and the parents anticipated their happy caregiving as she grew. Within a day, the head nurse in the nursery remarked, "That one is going to be trouble." The baby was unpredictable in feeding and sleeping and always seemed to be screaming. Unfortunately, the head nurse's gloomy prediction was all too accurate. For the following months, the child's behavior was a nightmare. Yet, both parents were experienced, and the two older daughters thrived and had no difficulties in their behavior. The pediatrician assured the parents that Jillian was normal, but they could find no explanations for her irregular schedule, the ease with which an upset escalated to loud tantrum, and difficulty in adjustment to any change.

Fortunately, a good friend, pediatrician and child psychiatrist Dr. Sol Nichtern, identified Jillian's problem as difficult temperament, and began to advise the parents on caregiving practices for such a child. The parents followed the advice, and by the time she was 2 years old Jillian's difficulty began to subside.

Turecki had previously read our first major book, *Temperament and Behavior Disorders in Children* (1968), with casual interest. Now, in 1976, he read the book carefully and began to understand temperament and its implications clearly. From the time Jillian's parents began to handle her in a manner that took into account her sensitivity to unfamiliar situations and her occasional tantrums, she began to flower and show strengths, such as a wonderful imagination. She became a joy to her parents and teachers, in contrast to her earlier years when she had been a source of almost constant turmoil, tension, and frustration in the family atmosphere (Turecki, with Torner, 1989).

With this experience with his daughter, and further familiarization with our books, Turecki decided that his conventional approach to his young patients, based on his standard training, was highly inadequate. Long, expensive treatment sessions had unsatisfactory results. With his characteristic energy, imagination, and thoughtfulness, Turecki transformed his professional life to focus on temperament issues.

In 1983, he started a clinic at Beth Israel Hospital for problem children with difficult temperament staffed by himself, a psychologist, and a social worker, under the joint sponsorship of the departments of psychiatry and pediatrics. The program grew quickly and the temperament program approach promised fast, positive results with the clinic patients.

Two later, in 1985, he wrote a book, *The Difficult Child*, to help parents to understand and manage hard-to-raise children. The book, based on our temperament findings and his clinic experiences, explains the categories and concepts lucidly, without jargon, and gives specific, clear advice to parents. His advice is sound, sensible, and practical and at the same time captures the essence of the vast amount of research in the area over the past 30 years. Turecki has made one change in our NYLS constellation of the "difficult child." He has defined the difficult child as a normal young child whose innate difficult temperament makes the child hard to raise for his or her particular family (Turecki, with Torner, 1989).

In 1986, he transformed his private practice to a private difficult child center, with its staff and criteria similar to those of the Beth Israel clinic he instituted in 1983. As in the clinic, his private cases have emphasized temperament based on parent guidance (Turecki, with Torner, 1989).

In summary, Turecki has made a major contribution through the establishment of a pioneering temperament clinic in a medical center, his valuable parent education book, and pointing to the importance of including temperament in the evaluation and treatment of children by psychiatrists in private practice. Unfortunately, Beth Israel Hospital developed financial problems in the late 1980s, as have so many hospitals, and the temperament clinic had to be phased out in 1989.

Turecki's private difficult child center continues, his book has been revised, and he lectures widely on the basic temperament issues to pediatricians and educators. He has started a detailed systematic follow-up of his clinic and private cases. This follow-up study could provide valuable objective findings to validate and expand the basic concepts of temperament programs (S. Turecki, personal communication, May 5, 1995).

The Minnesota Program

In 1976 the Minnesota legislative mandated and funded pilot Early Childhood Family Education Programs (ECFE) for 22 school districts. Each district was allowed to design a program to fit the community. Services included the choices of parent–child classes, home visits, family field trips, family fun times, book and toy lending libraries, and more. With succeeding years the programs were expanded to more school districts. By 1986 the program became available in 370 out of 420 school districts in the state.

Kurcinka's career in the family programs

Mary Kurcinka obtained a master's degree in "family social science" and in "family education" in 1977 at the University of Minnesota, and became licensed as both a parent educator and an early childhood educator by the state. She started her career in 1976 by developing one of the first of the pilot programs. She worked with this program until she was put in charge of one of the programs of the fourth largest school districts in the state. As has been true in most of the school districts, parent–child classes have served as the core of the program. The classes typically lasted 2 to 2 1/2 hours, the session including time for parents and children to interact, practice skills, and have fun.

In her academic training, Kurcinka was introduced to the concept of temperament and its application through our books and became impressed by its importance. As director of her school district program, she introduced the issue of temperament and encouraged parents to learn about their own temperament and that of their children. The parents focused on how to establish realistic expectations for their child's adaptation and to foster a better goodness of fit between parent and child.

Kurcinka's teaching and writing

Her teaching of temperament in the parents' school quickly became a stimulus for broader influence. She is a gifted teacher, and began lecturing in 1984 at a number of the other school district programs. Soon she began to receive requests to lecture from parenting groups outside of Minnesota with a gradually expanding audience.

From her lecturing experiences, Kurcinka, in 1991, wrote a superb book, *Raising Your Spirited Child.* She preferred the label "spirited" rather than "difficult." She has utilized our nine temperamental categories, changing some of the terms to reflect a positive aspect. For example, distractibility became perceptiveness and approach/ withdrawal to first reaction and sensory threshold became sensitivity. Her language is lively, lucid, good-humored, with a positive view of children and parents. At the same time, though, the content is thorough and accurate, with simple sensitive suggestions and rules for the parents. Her book has been a great success and at this writing, has sold almost 150,000 copies.

Calling Kurcinka a gifted teacher is a gross understatement. We heard her at the Kaiser Permanente temperament program in Oakland, California, in October 1994. In one session she spoke for an hour, demonstrating her typical presentation of temperament issues to the audience. She is attractive, with a charming smile and a clear, almost musical, and modulated voice, and is truly charismatic. She used several graphic illustrations and interjected humorous examples and vignettes, although her content was basically both serious and optimistic, as she explained the basic themes of how to know your child and how to manage the difficulties of a spirited child.

The audience, including us, was spellbound listening to her. It is no surprise that she has so many invitations from a wide variety of audiences and geographic areas. Since 1994 she has given an average of two lectures a week. Her audiences average two hundred attendees, and include groups at the Academy of Pediatrics, child-care professionals, nurses and health professionals, and families with children. She consistently impresses the professionals with the importance of temperament, and the curriculum of temperament is widely accepted in her Minnesota school district program.

Kurcinka is currently writing a second book, based on the kinds of questions and problems raised by her audiences. We are confident this second book will be as successful, and perhaps an even greater contribution to professional and family education to the field of temperament.

The Kaiser Permanente Program

The Kaiser Permanente health maintenance organization (HMO) is the oldest and largest in the country. It has established a unique and innovative temperament program for its families. The quantitative and qualitative findings of the program, actually still in its infancy, show that it is already making a valuable contribution. The program is so extensive in its scope and breadth that it merits a separate chapter, which follows.

13

THE KAISER PERMANENTE TEMPERAMENT PROGRAM

The Kaiser Permanente health maintenance organization is the first, the largest, and probably the best HMO in the United States. Their membership in the 11 regions around the United States is 6.5 million, with about 5 million of those shared between northern and southern California. It runs its own clinics and hospitals and emphasizes preventive programs, such as prenatal monitoring and vaccinations of young children.

In the early 1980s, Dr. David Rosen, a child psychiatrist who was chief of psychiatry at the San Rafael facility of Kaiser Permanente, north of San Francisco, met Dr. James Cameron, executive director of the Preventive Ounce, a nonprofit preventive mental health organization in Oakland, California. They were both familiar with our joint writings on temperament. They both saw the importance of a temperament program using parent guidance in the prevention of temperament-based behavior problems as well as early intervention with children who had already developed such temperament-related problems. In 1984, Drs. Cameron and Rice, both psychologists, developed infant and preschool temperament questionnaires based on our NYLS categories and devised computer software for scoring them and calculating a temperament profile. At the same time, Cameron trained a developmental psychologist, Jan Kristal, M.A., to function as a temperament counselor at Kaiser San Rafael, where she would be available to both parents and pediatricians regarding temperament issues.

DETAILS OF THE TEMPERAMENT PROGRAM

With this preliminary work, Rosen and Cameron developed an innovative temperament guidance program for parents of infants and toddlers at Kaiser Permanente San Rafael. Initially referred to as the Temperament-Based Anticipatory Guidance Program, it is now simply called the Temperament Program. When infants born to Kaiser Permanente mothers reach 4 months of age, the mother is sent a temperament questionnaire with a letter explaining the purpose of the program and requesting the mother fill out the form and mail it back to the Preventive Ounce for processing. Of the initial 1,641 forms sent out, approximately 30% were returned.

Each filled-in questionnaire was computer scored and generated a temperament profile for each child. For each infant, the computer program identified specific childcare issues (such as sleep, mealtime, or separation problems) that were more likely to occur per infant in the 5–6, 7–8, 9–10, and 11–12 month periods, based on probability calculations derived from a database of over one thousand HMO infants followed from 4 to 16 months in an earlier study at another HMO setting (Cameron & Rice, 1986).

Three quarters of the mothers received a letter spelling out the infant's temperament profile, with detailed parental advice emphasizing the normalcy of their child's unique temperament. In keeping with the goodness of fit concept, suggestions were made for constructive responses by the parents to their child's particular temperament. The remaining mothers (the control group) received no anticipatory guidance. For both experimental and control groups, a copy of the infant's temperament profile was placed in the medical chart (Cameron, Rice, Hansen, & Rosen, 1989).

Formal and informal follow-ups were conducted between 5 and 16 months of infant age. Informal conversations indicated that the facility's pediatricians were delighted with the effects of the anticipatory guidance. A substantial part of their clinical practice involved responding to parents' questions and problems about how to handle the various routines of the children's caretaking—sleeping, adapting to new foods, assertiveness problems. The anticipatory guidance saved time by reducing repeat telephone calls and office visits for the same problem. For both issue occurrence and management difficulty, the pattern of correlations matched those from previous studies (Cameron, Hansen, & Rosen, 1989).

Formal follow-up of the anticipatory predications were conducted at 8, 12, and 16 months of infant age. Both experimental and control group parents completed questionnaires asking what issues occurred in six behavioral areas (sleep problems, separation issues, accident risks, assertiveness problems, mealtime difficulties, and special sensitivities). If any issues did occur, parents were also asked how difficult they were to understand and manage.

For both experimental and control groups, 4-month temperament scale scores were significantly correlated to the occurrence of temperament-related behavioral issues in 13 of the 18 parental ratings, with p values ranging from .05 to .001. Twelve similar correlations with management difficulty items were statistically significant, again from .05 to .001 (Cameron, Rice, Rosen, & Chesterman, in submission).

Once the anticipatory guidance program and its temperament counselor were in place in the pediatric department, pediatricians could ask the temperament counselor

to mail out appropriate questionnaires for children ages
1 1/2 to 12 years, if they identified possible temperament-
related issues during their clinic visits. In addition to an-
swering the items on the temperament questionnaire, parents were asked to list their issues of current concern. In
the light of the temperament profile, the facility's temperament counselor reviewed the parent's behavioral concerns and made recommendations for issue management
directly to the parents or school, or through the child's
pediatrician (Cameron et al., 1994).

With both the anticipatory guidance and consultative
components of the Temperament Program, Kaiser Permanente pediatricians could offer specific and concrete recommendations for each child, making their counseling to
the parents both easier and more accurate. The pediatricians reported their positive response to the Kaiser Permanente administration, alerting them to this new program for the prevention of and early intervention with
childhood behavioral problems, in keeping with Kaiser
Permanente's philosophy of preventive medicine.

By 1991, the administration decided to go ahead with
substantial financial support for Cameron and Rosen's
program. With this help, they expanded the program to
enlist an increasing number of northern California Kaiser
facilities. By 1994, over half of the 30 northern California
Kaiser facilities were involved in the Temperament Program. On October 18–19, 1994, a conference was held in
Berkeley, California, to present the results of the temperament study and to train additional temperament counselors. The conference included a number of speakers (including ourselves), parent roundtable discussions, role-
playing of typical clinical vignettes, and an "Introduction
to Temperament Counseling" training manual. Similar
yearly training conferences are being planned.

Since the conference, the chiefs of pediatrics in northern California Kaiser voted to implement the Temperament Program throughout the entire region. In addition,
Rosen and Cameron have begun meeting with pediatri-

cians from other Kaiser Permanente regions and have started training several of these departments. They have been funded by the Garfield Memorial Fund to disseminate the Temperament Program to all 11 regions.

With the rapid expansion of the Temperament Program, Rosen relinquished his psychiatric position at his San Rafael HMO, and assumed the full-time position as director of the program. His prime activity involves dissemination of the program in an increasing number of the HMOs, with assistance in planning, training, and monitoring of these facilities (D. Rosen, personal communication, November 10, 1995).

THE TEACHING VIDEOTAPES

Soon after the 1994 conference, Cameron and Rosen completed the production of four teaching videotapes through Kaiser Permanente's audiovisual department. Their first videotape is an introduction to temperament concepts for parents, focused on the concept of temperament and its categories. Each of the other three tapes describes one of the three clusters of temperament characteristics that the research at Kaiser showed are most likely to result in temperament-based behavior problems, and includes recommendations for management. Written material will be provided as specific supplement for each videotape. (The videotapes can be requested by writing to the Temperament Program, Health Education Department, Kaiser Permanente, 1950 Franklin St., Oakland, CA, 94612.)

In the past year I (S.C.) have shown the tapes at various pediatric and child psychiatry units and academic centers where I was invited. This experience actually surprised me. The response to the tapes was universal stimulation and even excitement, in comparison to my other experiences with interesting but relatively mild response to my lecturing over the years.

Of special importance, Cameron, Rice, Hansen, and Rosen have launched into an objective study to demonstrate the cost-effectiveness of temperament-based anticipatory guidance. In a study of medical visits made to one Kaiser Permanente facility in northern California, parents who received written anticipatory guidance for their infant at 4 months were found to use 1.5 fewer medical visits for their child in the subsequent year than parents who did not receive such guidance.

With approximately 24,000 live births a year in the northern California Kaiser Permanente region and a parental participation rate now of 35% in this anticipatory guidance program regionwide, the savings in pediatric, family practice, and emergency room visits is estimated at over 12,000 visits annually. This translates into net savings of $700,000 over the cost of the program, just in northern California (Cameron, Rice, Hansen, and Rosen, 1994).

Beyond this analysis of cost-effectiveness, recent Kaiser Permanente studies by Cameron and colleagues pinpoint why temperament-based anticipatory advice is clinically effective. They found that parents of firstborns who are more temperamentally difficult (more active, slower adjusting) reported greater understanding and acceptance of their child after receiving their anticipatory guidance than did parents of easier children. By contrast, with the parents who did not receive the guidance, apparently infant behavior that can't be understood and seen as normal created parental anxiety and dissonance, leading to repeated medical visits to fix "what's wrong."

EXPANSION OF THE PROGRAM TO A
PSYCHIATRIC DEPARTMENT

As for the cost-effectiveness of the consultation service provided by the Temperament Program, Rosen reported that in his facility's psychiatry department began to send temperament questionnaires to parents who had requested psychiatric evaluations as a result of children's behavior problems. The therapist then discussed the temperament profile with the parents, and the possible temperament basis of the child's problem was advised. As the time of this writing, Rosen reports that approximately 25% of the parents that came to him with concerns about their children did not require further visits after receiving the temperament information. They felt they now understood the child's behavior and how to manage it (D. Rosen, personal communication, November, 1995).

PERSPECTIVE

As a final note, another large HMO system (CIGNA health plan) has become interested in the program pioneered at Kaiser Permanente and recently has adopted the anticipatory guidance program for 4-month-olds throughout its facilities in the Phoenix, Arizona, region. Other HMOs, from Group Health Cooperative of Puget Sound to the Harvard Community Health Plan, have also expressed interest. With the tremendous expansion of managed care in the past few years, preventive programs that can reduce medical visits and satisfy parents will become even more important. In that environment, temperament-based consulting and anticipatory guidance has the potential to become a standard part of pediatric and psychiatric health care.

14

A NEW MENTAL HEALTH PROFESSION: THE TEMPERAMENT COUNSELOR

In Chapter 9, parent guidance was defined as a valuable treatment strategy in child psychiatry, as "the formulation of a program of altered functioning by the parents that could ameliorate excessive and harmful stress from the child."

The chapter spelled out the rationale of this treatment approach when the cause of a child's behavioral disturbance was created by a poorness of fit between the parents' undesirable demands and expectations and the child's specific temperamental traits. In such cases a sequence of counseling steps was required to achieve a modification of the parents' attitude so as to change to a goodness of fit from a poorness of fit.

THE TEMPERAMENT COUNSELOR

The leaders of the temperament programs in La Grande, Oregon (Chapter 12) and in California (Chapter 13) hit on the same idea. A specific director of the therapeutic team,

111

whether a psychiatrist, pediatrician, or clinical director, was required. But the specific therapist for the procedures of the parent guidance, whether a social worker, nurse, or educator, did not necessarily require formal degrees, but rather to be trained in parent guidance skills. The essential skill required was a thorough grasp of the concept of temperament, the definitions of the categories of temperament, and the functional assets and difficulties for each trait, and familiarity with the concept of a good or poor fit in each parent–child interaction. Above all, a parent counselor needed the skillfulness and talent to communicate these effectively to the parents in a positive parent–counselor session.

The program leaders anticipated that these counselors could be successfully trained within a relatively short period of time and could be from a variety of professional or even nonprofessional fields. As indicated in previous chapters, the Kaiser Permanente program with a trained psychologist, the La Grande program with parents, and the program at the Arizona State University with nurses (Chapter 17) have achieved competent temperament counselors.

THE KAISER PERMANENTE TEMPERAMENT COUNSELORS

Because the Kaiser Permanente (K.P.) training program has been the largest and most extensive development of the training of counselors, our focus will be on the lessons and implications of this program.

Jan Kristal, M.A.

In 1986, Dr.Cameron trained the first K.P. temperament counselor, the developmental psychologist Jan Kristal, at the San Rafael HMO, where she would be available to both parents and pediatricians. At the same time, Jan was enrolled as a graduate psychology student at San Francisco State University, from which she received her M.A. in 1990.

During her graduate years, she gave several lectures to the child development students. Her professor was impressed by Jan's lectures and suggested that it might be possible and desirable to introduce a course on temperament in the department. Jan was delighted and began to work up a syllabus for such a course. We reviewed her syllabus outline, were impressed, and encouraged her with some suggestions. By now, she has done a draft of over one hundred pages, and we will review it with her for a final draft. Her professor has approved the announcement of the course for next year, entitled "Understanding Individual Developments in Children's Temperament." Once the course, with her complete syllabus, is started, it will represent a pioneering, substantial training resource for temperament counselors.

Jan also has developed workshops on temperament for teachers, both preschool and elementary school. She sees an increasing interest in individuals training as temperament counselors. Now Jan and another HMO counselor in the area have raised the possibility of organizing a private counseling center, which they would call a Temperament Learning Center. This idea reflects their enthusiasm for the value of parent guidance, but she is realistic enough to know that she must first discover whether such a training center would be feasible. She is exploring the nitty-gritty problems of such an idea—credentials, curriculum, requirements for the students, budget, and so on.

Jan has worked actively in the San Rafael HMO temperament program. Almost all of the cases are referred by the pediatricians, and when a parent guidance routine is completed, she reports the findings back to the pediatrician. She has not tabulated the findings of her case records, but estimates that for 80% the results are successful, and that parent guidance usually requires three to four sessions. As to be expected, her cases are similar to

those we presented in Chapters 8 and 9. Even with successful parent guidance for the infancy or preschool
childhood years, at later developmental stages (early
school child, etc.) new demands may produce new symptoms, and require a new period of counseling. As to be
expected in any psychiatric practice, some cases can be
very frustrating for a temperament counselor if the parent
is not cooperative or has other complicating issues. In
such cases the parent may have to be referred to the psychiatric unit.

Other Temperament Counselor Training

Beyond the training activities Jan Kristal has been developing, this project has also included the overall education of the K.P. Temperament Program by Drs. Cameron
and Rosen in their involvement in an increasing number
of the HMO units. They have first concentrated on the
development of temperament programs in 13 K.P. HMO
units in northern California. This unit has trained temperament counselors with varied backgrounds—nine nurses,
two psychologists, and two physicians (Cameron, et al.,
1994). Dr. Rosen has committed his professional time to
educating the HMO units in different geographical areas
and has included the training of temperament counselors.
From the positive responses he has received to his visits
at succeeding units, he is planning for a sequential large
number of the units, (D. Rosen, personal communication,
November 10, 1995).

A PROBLEM FOR THE EXPANSION OF
TEMPERAMENT COUNSELORS

We can anticipate that there will be an increasing number of professionals and nonprofessionals interested in
becoming temperament counselors as a result of the flood
of books, articles, lectures, and workshops in these past

few years. Jan Kristal tells us that she has heard from personal communications that this is actually beginning to happen.

We are concerned that various people will begin to call themselves temperament counselors in private practice without adequate training or credentials. There is a danger of harm to children and a backlash for the field. We plan to communicate these issues and their solution to our colleagues and officers of the appropriate professional organizations.

15

TEMPERAMENT AND SCHOOL FUNCTIONING

With the onset of formal schooling, a new and more complex hierarchy of demands and expectations begins to influence the child's psychological development. The elementary school, high school, and higher educational settings become new centers of challenge, adaptation, and mastery for the individual's development.

The school makes a number of new demands on the student that include the mastery of increasingly complex cognitive tasks and the simultaneous requirements to adapt to a new geographic setting, to strange adults in unfamiliar roles, and to a host of new rules and regulations. Peer group activities in school become more elaborate and challenging.

Temperament plays an important role in shaping the course of school functioning. This influence is part of a highly complex interaction in comparison with the simple dynamic goodness-of-fit issues in infancy and the preschool period. Temperamental characteristics will help shape the individual student's mastery of new and demanding cognitive school functioning, but so will the student's intellectual and perceptual capacities, level of motivation, and psychodynamic patterns, as well as teacher characteristics, curriculum structure, and nature of peer social relations in school.

Basically, the significant issues of temperament will be emphasized in this chapter, as in the book as a whole.

CASE ILLUSTRATIONS

A limited number of case vignettes indicate the scope and variety of situations in which one or another temperamental characteristic can influence a child's school functioning.

Easy Temperament

As to be expected, most easy children had no difficulty in adjusting quickly and cheerfully to all the school-age levels. But, there were always a few exceptions. Isobel, a child of above average intelligence who had previously learned with ease, became an increasingly poor student in second grade. It was at this point that a consultation was requested by her parents. On the surface, it appeared that this child, despite her easy temperament, had not adapted to her school's academic standard.

Once the parents' own personal histories were explored, the reason for the problem became apparent. The parents had their own special high standard of uniqueness, of the right of each person to be individual—a commendable principle. They encouraged self-expression in the child, and Isobel, with easy temperament, quickly learned the parental standards in the preschool years. However, with her 7-year-old cognitive processes and her delight in being unique, she interpreted her parents' message in a way that they had not intended in the school environment. She was unwilling to take the necessary routine teaching procedure from the teacher. When engaged in dramatic play, Isobel was outstanding in her creative imagination, but she did not consider the teacher's directions to be her concern and expected individualized instruction for herself. With this attitude, she learned little and her educational level progressively diminished. Simultaneously, she also began to disregard the standard rules in play with her peer groups at school, proposing her own more creative judgments. Inevitably, she became unpopular and extruded by the group's social activities, much to her bewilderment.

When I interpreted how this problem had developed, the parents understood it immediately. They were dedicated parents who were completely committed to Isobel's healthy development. They were pleased at how easily Isobel had learned their value standards, but had no idea that she would interpret this inappropriately for her academic and social development. In other words, Isobel had a good fit with her parents' expectations, but a poor fit with the school's demands. My advice to the parents was clear and simple. They should try to teach Isobel the selectivity of their creative message. She should certainly maintain her appreciation of creative individuality, with the recognition that there were circumstances in which it was appropriate to accept and adapt to the reasonable rules and expectations of all kinds of environmental situations. The parents understood and embraced my suggestions immediately, and proceeded gently and firmly to teach Isobel how to expand her repertoire of positive academic and social behaviors. She learned quickly, didn't change her sense of being an individual, and within a year Isobel's school grades were high and she had become a popular member of her peer group.

Difficult Temperament

Carl was very different in temperament and school career from Isobel. In his early infancy he was rated as one of the most temperamentally difficult children in our NYLS sample. Whether it was the first bath, his first solid food, first birthday party, or the like, each new experience evoked from Carl rejection with loud and persistent crying. It almost seemed fated that a poorness of fit would

develop. Indeed, his mother's reaction was to feel both
helpless and personally guilty, with snatches of angry
feelings at Carl's behavior. Fortunately, his father's attitude provided both goodness of fit for Carl and much
needed respite for his wife.

The father, in his childhood and adult years, had a
quiet and peaceful personality. No matter how upset,
angry, happy, or delighted he was, his outward expressiveness remained calm. He had always envied his
friends and others who could burst out with stormy expressions of feeling at outrage or injustice. And, now, he
had a son, Carl, who was a tough young child to handle,
but who could become the kind of person he admired.
The father was delighted when Carl became a miniature
tornado or shouted with pleasure. He called Carl lusty,
praised him, and dealt patiently and calmly with Carl's
episodes of acute distress. As marriages are said to be
"made in heaven," this could be said about the goodness
of fit between Carl and his father.

The mother, on the other hand, could not duplicate her
husband's handling, although she tried. She was convinced that Carl's difficult behavior was her fault, in spite
of her husband's and our reassurances, and she was so
burdened with guilt that she sought help in a course of
psychotherapy.

The father, in his quiet, reasonable way, was the domi-
nant member of the family, considerate of his wife yet
adamant that, despite its inconvenience, he saw no reason
to wish that Carl should change his temperament. Also,
the mother's guilty self-recrimination didn't require a
long course of therapy. Actually, her most effective therapy was the realization that year by year Carl's difficult
behavior became less evident as he gradually adapted
positively to so many routine and basic circumstances.

Without the need for any formal parent guidance from
us, the father handled his son so successfully that by the
time Carl's early first difficulties had been successfully
surmounted, he did well in school, and made a number

of good friends. An observer of Carl's functioning in his middle childhood and high school years, without the knowledge of the history of his early years, might well have classified him as belonging in the easy temperament group. Except for an occasional eruption with some totally new circumstance, there seemed to be no remnant of difficult temperament.

The years passed while Carl progressed academically, expanded his positive special activities, and maintained his family's harmonious pattern. When Carl was 18 he called me (S.C.) for an appointment to discuss his problems. He was puzzled and troubled about his unexpected problems. These had emerged when he had started college six months earlier. He had been eager to go and described eager and confident anticipation of his new life. But all his expectations were shattered by a reaction that was unexpected and contrary to his high school style of functioning. He found studying difficult and made virtually no friends. He was completely bewildered by his discomfort and isolation and kept repeating "This just isn't me!" I reviewed the possible causes for his problem—loss of dependency on his parents, sexual conflict, overwhelming academic demands, peer competitions. I found no evidence for any of these stresses. Fortunately, I was familiar with his history from infancy in his routine NYLS records. He had been a difficult child, with intense stressful responses to new situations, but he had had the opportunity to master each new demand gradually with support from his father, teachers, and friends. He had lived in the same community, had gone through the schools with his schoolmates and friends, and new subjects had been introduced gradually. He had come to view himself as an easily adaptable person.

When he entered college the story was different. Instead of his gradual adaptations over the years, he was now confronted with a whole series of new, demanding situations. He had to adapt to an unfamiliar new environment, he had to find new friends in this college, and his

classes required a new and different approach to schedules, curricula, teaching methods, and expectations from
his professors. His high school adaptation did not apply.
Despite his high motivation, with his temperamental
characteristics he could not adapt quickly and positively
to so many demanding new experiences at once. Despite
this culture shock, his years of successful coping had
built up self-confidence and a positive self-image, which
he was determined to regain. His parents, particularly his
father, had the insight to suggest that he utilize the resources of the NYLS by calling me. Carl had indeed been
unexpectedly faced with a need for a crash course in temperamental self-awareness and the devising of techniques
for familiarization with these multiple expectations so as
to turn stress into mastery.

I needed only one discussion with Carl. My explanation
of his disturbed behavior made immediate sense to him.
He began to take steps—temporarily reduced the number
of new courses, utilized his temperamental long attention
span and persistence to regular hard study. He also made
a point of attending his schoolmates' social activities, no
matter how tense he felt.

I saw Carl again at the end of the academic year, his
problems had disappeared, and he had recouped the positive academic and social standing of his high school
years. He was planning to transfer to another college for
good academic reasons, and I cautioned him that he might
have similar difficulties in the beginning of his new college, or, for that matter, in any unexpected combination
of new experiences in the future. His response was
"That's all right. I know how to handle them now." And
Carl was right. There have been several subsequent interviews in the 15 interviewing years. He has forged ahead
successfully in his academic preparations, work, and social activities.

Slow-to-Warm-Up Temperament

Barbara was typically slow-to-warm-up from early infancy. Her nursery school adaptation was stressful and

slow, but handled well by her mother and teacher. With her succeeding positive adaptation in nursery school and kindergarten, she started first grade easily and, being a bright child, forged ahead toward the top of the class with her reading scores. With this impressive record, the teacher advanced Barbara to the third year class. Our NYLS staff school interviewer reviewed the details of Barbara's school year functioning. During the first few months, Barbara had had real difficulty in mastering the third grade curriculum, and the teacher questioned whether the decision to advance her from the first to the third grade had been advisable.

The teacher expressed her concern to Barbara's mother and suggested that a second grade curriculum was more suited to her ability. The mother said, "I know Barbara. She could do the third year curriculum successfully. But she is a girl who always needs time to cope with any new situation. By being accelerated to the third grade, she has been faced with strange classmates and a different level of learning curriculum. From our experience with Barbara, if we are patient, she will gradually adjust herself and by Christmas you'll see, she will be a good student." The teacher then told the interviewer, "You know, when Barbara's mother predicted that time was all that was needed, I told myself that this was one more family that was placing excessive academic stress on their child. Mostly, I was skeptical with such explanations, but for Barbara's mother, I somehow felt her suggestion deserved a chance as she didn't seem to be that type of person. Reluctantly, I kept Barbara in my class, and you know, her mother was perfectly right. By Christmas, Barbara showed genuine mastery of her academic tasks, and now, at the end of the year, she is one of our top pupils, and helps other children with their work."

Low Activity Level

Kathy, one of the NYLS sample, had a marked slowness in her physical pace. In kindergarten, she was ridiculed as the "slowpoke" by her classmates and also became the butt of the teacher's impatience. The teacher labeled Kathy as "sluggish" and probably intellectually slow. The teacher reluctantly promoted her; it was only from kindergarten to the first grade. The new teacher quickly felt this promotion had been a mistake because Kathy was so "slow and plodding."

After the first conference with the parents, the teacher expressed her misgivings, saying that she might have to recommend Kathy to a special retarded class. The parents were both alarmed and confused. It was also true at home that Kathy was slow in her movements, but she was always reliable and responsible in their family rules and routines, and somehow they couldn't believe that Kathy was retarded. The parents arranged for a consultation with me (S.C.) to evaluate the reason for Kathy's apparent problems.

All our NYLS subjects had been routinely given IQ tests by our staff psychologist. Kathy, whose test had been done just 6 months before, had scored at a low average IQ level. The psychologist felt Kathy could have done much better if her test responses had not been done so slowly. I tested Kathy myself with a number of cognitive tasks and game activities. Although she thought slowly, her responses were alert and accurate. I told the parents Kathy had no intellectual deficit at all. Actually, I was impressed that her cognitive abilities and motor dexterity were actually above average. She should not be called "slow," but rather "deliberate," a trait that is often desirable. I gave this report to the teacher and advised her and the parents to be patient with Kathy and praise her for her frequent successful completion of tasks and activities. If they did this, Kathy's positive self-esteem would mature, and her classmates and other friends would begin to respect her, no longer as the "slowpoke," but rather as reliable and contemplative. Fortunately, the teacher was a sensitive and thoughtful professional, and understood my findings, and carried through these recommendations. By the end of the year Kathy had learned up to grade level, this positive judgment was passed on to succeeding teachers, and she mastered easily and deliberately each year her academic and social school functioning.

Summary

These vignettes describe academic situations in which the knowledge of a child's temperamental individuality was the key to the selection of an intervention designed to free the child of excessive stress and permit optimum functioning. In each of these examples, the nature of the stress was specific to the nature of the temperamental characteristics; in each a youngster of different temperament would have been free of stress. The interventions, while requiring modification of parents' and/or teacher's attitudes at the time of problem identification, had, as a hallmark of their success, the youngsters' ability to master the once stressful demands.

Such successful guidance advice was useful to the teachers who were committed to the welfare of their pupils. Unfortunately, some teachers who were inflexible and even incompetent could label a child as "bad" or "willful" or the parents as "undisciplined" or "at fault" for the child's behavior, or both. We can remember the tragedies when some teachers or parents refused to truly understand this and modify any inflexible approach that inevitably led to a child's disastrous life and school developmental course.

SYSTEMATIC STUDIES OF TEMPERAMENT AND SCHOOL FUNCTIONING

The vignettes above are a limited sampling of the large number of children in the NYLS cohort whose temperaments played an important role in shaping the course of school functioning. This clinical judgment has been con-

firmed by a number of systematic and objective studies
by experienced research educators. The most definitive
studies have been done by Dr. Barbara Keogh, professor
of education at UCLA, and her colleagues Michael Pullis
and Joel Cadwell, and by Dr. Roy Martin, professor of educational psychology at the University of Georgia. Their
studies have been done with large numbers of students
and teachers. Their findings have been extensive and impressive and will be summarized briefly.

Keogh devised and used a shortened form of our
Teacher Temperament Questionnaire (Thomas and
Chess, 1977) and then factored out her pupils' questionnaire data with three primary dimensions: Task Orientation (persistence, distractibility, and activity); Personal
Social Flexibility (approach/withdrawal, positive mood,
and adaptability); and Reactivity (negative mood, sensory
threshold, and intensity). Ratings were determined of the
teachers' "teachability," that is, teachers' decisions about
classroom management and placement recommendations. Keogh (1982) found a strong and consistent relationship between temperamental characteristics, especially Task Orientation, and teachers' classroom
decisions (teachability). In addition, teachers overesti-
mated the learning ability of pupils with specific temperamental characteristics such as Flexibility. She summarized that the variations in temperamental patterns "are
clear contributors to teachers' views of pupils' teachability, to the estimate they make of pupils' abilities, and to
the kind of expectations they have from pupils' educational performance. Recognition of the stylistic differences in children's behavior is important for teachers, as
their variations are the basis of many instructional and
management decisions" (Keogh, 1982, p. 278).

In a separate study in a small school district in Illinois,
Pullis and Cadwell (1982) basically duplicated Keogh's
methods. They expanded her study by calculating a re-
gression equation controlling for ratings of ability, motivation, and social interaction studies. Their findings es-

sentially confirmed those of Keogh and they reached similar conclusions.

Roy Martin (1982) and his coworkers have done a substantial series of studies of the correlations between the child's temperament and various aspects of the child's school functioning. They used a modified instrument of our Teacher Temperament Questionnaire and correlated its data with pupil scholastic achievement. In their four careful studies, important relations between the traits of activity, distractibility and persistence, and scholastic ability were identified.

In the 1970s and 1980s an extensive body of literature by a number of investigators was accumulated consisting of studies of the relationship between temperament and the school. Keogh (1989) reviewed these reports comprehensively and systematically. At the conclusion of her review she summarizes a number of pertinent comments on psychoeducational assessment and implications for teachers (Keogh 1989, pp. 444–446).

In Keogh's earlier paper (1982), she made a cogent comment: "Teachers who have participated in our research have reported that consideration of pupils' temperament has made them more sensitive to their own perception of individual children" (Keogh 1982, p. 277). Her observation has strongly confirmed our own experience, gained both from the yearly subjects' teacher interviews of the NYLS protocol and in our own many discussions with teachers from many different schools in clinical settings. With few exceptions, teachers have grasped quickly the concepts of temperamental individuality and its application to the concept of goodness of fit. The teachers have told us and our staff interviewers that their application of temperament to individual pupils has made their teaching activities more effective and even easier.

16

TEMPERAMENT AND PEDIATRIC PRACTICE

During the early decades of our NYLS program, our concepts and findings attracted various professionals involved with basic child development issues. It was especially the pediatricians who thoughtfully, and even enthusiastically, embraced our NYLS reports and the significance of their implications.

The successor of Benjamin Spock, the famous American family pediatrician Barry Brazelton, at Harvard, commented that "Stella Chess and Alexander Thomas had made it 'de rigeur' to think of different styles of development in children" (Brazelton, 1969, p. xx).

As one example, I (A.T.) had an unexpected compliment from a solo private practice pediatrician in a small town in South Carolina. In the late 1970s, a good friend, a widower, had remarried a southern woman, a widow, with several adolescent children. My friend called me, told me that one of his stepsons had had several unusual acute episodes of behavioral disturbance, and asked me to evaluate the youngster's problem. I set the appointment for the child together with his mother. Both described the episodes of rather bizarre aggressive behaviors that appeared suddenly and then disappeared within a few hours. At the consultation my detailed questions and observations and a superficial neurological examination could not identify any significant evidence of any continuing abnormal behavior, or of any specific special stress in his current or early life. The mother confirmed the son's story and the overall character of his functioning.

The diagnosis was not at all clear, but suggested the possibility of an epileptic equivalent disorder. As to his early years, I could not elicit from him or his mother any childhood symptoms of an epileptic equivalent. He had grown up in a small southern town where he had received his pediatric care. I therefore phoned this pediatrician and identified myself. He interrupted me with excitement, "Dr. Thomas, I am honored to finally tell you and Dr. Chess that you have made such a great difference in my understanding of my patients' problems, and being able to treat them so much better. I just must thank the both of you deeply." I was deeply gratified and complimented him on keeping in touch so well with new developments in the field. I then explained the cause for my call. The pediatrician looked up his file and told me that the boy had a perfectly normal development and never had any suspicion of an epileptic equivalent in his behavior through his childhood.

I told the youngster and mother I could not find any abnormalities in my examination, and suggested we wait and see if any further attacks occurred. If so, I would recommend him for a thorough neurological examination and testing. As it happened, after this consultation, to my knowledge, the youngster never had an attack or any other significant pathological behavior.

At another level, with the Kaiser Permanente HMO temperament program, as described in a former chapter, it was impressive how the large pediatric staffs of the HMOs had uniformly understood quickly and were ready to apply the findings and recommendations of the temperament program.

Other professionals have accepted our concepts and findings relatively slowly. But, it was the pediatricians who responded positively and quickly.

WISDOM OF THE PEDIATRICIANS

From their own functioning, pediatricians know that babies from birth onward are different in their behavior. They get to recognize these differences as they take care of their child patients, and use this knowledge in making their decisions as to diagnosis and treatment of each child who comes into their office with a complaint or symptom. One child who comes in crying loudly with a sprained ankle has always strongly objected to any routine procedure, whether done by an injection or even simply using a tongue depressor. The doctor remembers this, examines the mildly swollen ankle, and decides the loud crying is in no way ominous, and simply straps the ankle and gives a small dose of aspirin. Another child who comes in quietly with a sprained ankle has always accepted the doctor's routine procedures with mild quick whimpers. With this child, the pediatrician notices she has tears and is restraining herself from crying. The twisted ankle is not more swollen than the other child's, but when asked "Does it hurt?" the youngster nods strongly but quietly. With this child the doctor is much more concerned over the sprained ankle than with the first, and orders an Xray of the ankle. And sure enough, the Xray shows a fracture of the ankle that requires an entirely different treatment for the child than the simple ankle strapping.

The Evaluation of the Mother

An astute pediatrician also estimates the idiosyncratic personality patterns of mothers. One mother who chronically leaves telephone messages that her child needs urgent attention, even for a mild fever or a scraped knee, may be the last one on the list of returned telephone messages. Another mother is relaxed, rarely worries over her child, and expects that the youngster with a mild pain or a rather badly scraped knee will get better without needing the doctor's attention. When the doctor comes to the

office, checks the list of telephone calls, and reads this
mother's message that "Bobby has had a pain on the lower
right side of his abdomen, is nauseous and has a fever
of 101 degrees. Should I do something or just leave him
alone?" With that message and that mother, the pediatrician responds immediately and arranges to examine the
child right away. The fact that she has a question immediately alerts the pediatrician to respond, and the nature of
her calm and organized information leads the doctor to
suspect that Bobby may have acute appendicitis.

When we started our NYLS with our hypothesis of the
functional significance of individual differences, we visited an old family friend, Dr. Lewis Fraad, professor and
chair of the department of pediatrics of a first-rate medical
school. We came to ask Lew about his judgment of our
hypothesis and our plan to test it with our research project. We, as everyone, deeply respected both Lew's clinical
and his research expertise, and took advantage of our
friendship to get his opinion. He laughed, "I'll tell you
what I do. Some of my patients' mothers bedevil me with
complaints that their children are fussy and difficult to
manage. I know that these children are normal and look
for some way to say so without seeming to ignore the
mothers' concerns. I tell the mother the child is going
through an Oedipal stage, it is normal, don't worry, and
the child will finally live through this stage. Of course, I
don't believe in this Oedipus nonsense, but the mothers
are impressed by my expert knowledge, feel that they
have gotten an explanation, and stop pestering me. And
as they relax, so do the children. I don't know what other
pediatricians do with such parents, but it works for me."

Then Lew turned to us and said, "Your hypothesis is
reasonable, and if you prove it through your research
study, that will be fine, and I won't have to talk about the
Oedipus complex again." We were amused and thanked
him. We were sure that his gimmick was fine, but we were
sure he would also immediately detect when a mother's

fussing signaled a possible real problem, and give attention to the child very quickly.

Dr. William B. Carey

In the 1960s Dr. William B. Carey, a young pediatrician in private practice in a suburb of Philadelphia, asked to meet with us. It was soon clear that he had a scholarly and inventive mind. He kept up with the various research programs in the field, and his attention had been caught strongly with one issue: temperament. He had been following our reports of the NYLS findings in our systematic study of temperament with its theoretical and practical implications. As an astute clinician, Carey quickly recognized that the applications of our theory and practical findings would augment the effectiveness of pediatric practice. He also estimated that the identification and rating of temperament categories, according to the details of our research NYLS protocol, would be impractical for a busy practitioner in his office or clinic. As a man of action, he set up the goal of devising a short questionnaire that could cover the essential temperamental categories and their ratings. He came to consult this plan with us. We were delighted with his proposal, which was totally compatible with our work. Carey then enlisted a colleague, Dr. Sean McDevitt, a psychologist with expertise in the development of quantitative models, including questionnaires. By 1968 both had developed a psychometrically sound infant questionnaire that required about 20 minutes for the parent to answer the questions, and about 10 minutes to score (Carey, 1970).

Carey reported this first questionnaire in 1970, and it was quickly picked up by an increasing number of clinicians and researchers who had been attracted to our evidence that temperament included a significant functional variable in healthy and deviant psychological development. Since then, Carey and his coworkers have developed questionnaires for 1- to 3-year old, 3- to 7-year-old, and 8- to 12-year-old children, which have all been widely used.

Not surprisingly, Carey's interest blossomed beyond the questionnaires, and to date he has published a series of almost 30 clinical pediatric papers. He attended a number of the special temperament conferences, and his comments, suggestions, and criticisms were always concise, incisive, and thoughtful. And, in any discussion, his wry humor was also always a pleasure.

Carey arranged to get together an international interdisciplinary group for a 5-day temperament meeting at the Lake Como conference center sponsored by the Rockfeller Foundation, and, together with McDevitt, edited the proceedings (Carey & McDevitt, 1989). He has coedited two editions of a comprehensive textbook, *Developmental-Behavioral Pediatrics* (Levine, Carey, & Crocker, 1992). After 31 years in general pediatric practice, Carey is now clinical professor of pediatrics at the University of Pennsylvania and is teaching and supervising in the behavioral pediatrics section of the Children's Hospital of Philadelphia.

Carey started as a simple private pediatrician—he used to say of himself, "I'm just a country doctor"—but with his fertile mind he realized the significance of temperament from our research reports. As he forged ahead with his colleague McDevitt, by leaps and bounds, one can only marvel at his productive contributions and his status as an authority not only in temperament but in the overall field of behavioral pediatrics. He is the last one to rest on his laurels. Carey and McDevitt (1995) have just now published a definitive book for professionals, *Coping With Children's Temperament*. Leading professionals characterize his books as follows: "This clear, logical book is a treasure house . . . There is no match for this book." "A wonderful, richly textured and highly readable book." We comment that "this is a splendid book," and add that Dr. Carey's pediatric work has indeed been a splendid career. And we are sure this book and his career so far are no more than the beginning, and we anticipate contributions for many years.

17

TEMPERAMENT AND NURSING PRACTICE

Two 9-year-old boys, Robert and Martin, from different families, were admitted to the same pediatric surgical unit on the same morning with acute appendicitis. That afternoon, each had a simple appendectomy without complications.

On the first postoperative morning the head nurse reviewed nursing needs with the student nurse, focusing her teaching on these two boys whom she herself had observed. The student nurse reported that Robert had been complaining loudly about pain in his incision and she thought that he needed a strong dose of pain medication. Martin, in contrast, was lying quietly awake making no commotion, so that he did not appear to need any pain relief. The charge nurse listened, smiled, and invited the student to accompany her while she checked the boys.

As they approached the beds, Robert was restless and looked cranky. As soon as he saw the nurses coming, he began to fuss loudly. In contrast, Martin was quiet. The charge nurse checked Robert's temperature and pulse, pulled back one end of the abdominal dressing to check the incision, and found it clean and neatly closed with no sign of infection. The nurse smiled and said, "Robby, you are doing fine. I'm sure that the operation hurts you a little, but I don't think you need to complain so much. Do you always fuss a lot when anything hurts you, like

if you scrape your knee a bit if you fall?" Robert looked
sheepish and said, "Yes, when I yell you can hear me all
over the house. My parents say they can't tell by my yell-
ing whether I bumped my elbow or broke my arm. But
they tell me I am really a good kid." The nurse laughed,
"Robby, I'm sure you're a good boy. Of course, your incision will hurt you a bit for another day or two, and we
will give you some medicine. Unless it really hurts a lot,
will you try to control your fussing? Otherwise it could
upset the other children nearby." Robert nodded.

The nurse turned to Martin, checked his pulse and temperature, and found both to be slightly elevated. She
looked at his incision, and found it a little red and swollen. She bent over Martin, smoothed his hair, and said
softly, "Marty, I think your incision must be hurting you.
You're a brave boy, but you must tell me." Martin nodded
quietly and then burst into tears. "It hurts me a lot and
I'm worried." The nurse comforted him, reassured him.
"Your operation is doing fine, you don't have to worry,
we will give you medicine for a day or two. You'll be
home soon, and in a week or two you'll be back to school
and joining your baseball team." Martin nodded and said,
"Thank you, I feel better already." Appropriate notations
were made on the chart to alert Martin's surgeon.

At the nurse's station the charge nurse reviewed the les-
son of this episode—in essence, that the nurse must assess each patient's individual medical needs and comfort.
The message of the appearances of the wounds and the
pulse and temperatures was clear and objective. But the
student nurse clearly had not been taught to understand
the specific meanings and messages of each patient's behavioral individuality. "Because Robert made a big fuss
over his pain, you thought he needed a high dose of medication. But a little inquiry showed that he behaved that
way about everything. All he needs now is a mild dose
and assurance. As to Martin, whose incision is slightly
inflamed, his failure to complain can mean many things,
including low sensitivity to pain or silent anxiety. You

saw how quietly he confided his pain and his worry when we took the time to ask. When his parents visit, we should inquire whether he is always so stoical and uncomplaining. It is easy to ignore the real needs of an uncomplaining patient who needs comfort and reassurance. But we could have missed the indication that his incision was beginning to become infected. In contrast to Robert, Martin needs a stronger dose of medication. We have to call the surgeon and report the danger of the infected incision, so that appropriate measures can be taken."

The charge nurse looked at the student, who was aghast at her misjudgments. She smiled, "You're still a student and have a lot to learn. Have your teachers assigned you the textbook by Whaley and Wong?" (1983). "No," the student answered, "I've heard about the book, but we haven't been assigned it." In that pediatric nursing textbook, the authors describe individual behavioral differences in children, called temperament. The authors discuss the ways in which understanding of temperament, which influences a child's behavior and development, can be applied as a practical tool by nurses. Martin and Robert are illustrations of this tool.

THE ROLE OF THE NURSE

Nurses are on the firing line all day and night with sick children or adults and with the anxious parents of healthy youngsters, whether in a hospital, clinic, school, or special institution. The clinical vignette cited just above is typical. An experienced and sensitive nurse knows how important it is to identify the individual differences in behavior that different children show. We have been impressed innumerable times over the years at how well nurses appreciate the importance of the formulation of temperament, whether they are familiar with the term itself or not, and how well they apply this concept in their daily work.

SYSTEMATIC NURSING STUDIES AND DISCUSSION

Progressive appreciation by experienced nurses of the importance of temperament has been reflected in the systematic studies and growing frequency of temperament discussions in nursing journals and textbooks, starting with the early 1980s (Chess & Thomas, 1986). This momentum in the early 1980s has by now been expanded by the growing number of contributions by nurse researchers and teachers.

Nancy Melvin, R.N., Ph.D., professor of nursing at Arizona State University, has been awarded a very substantial 3-year grant from the National Institute for Nursing Research with her project titled "Children's Temperament: Nursing Intervention for Parents." Several expert temperament researchers (including S.C.) are acting as consultants on the project.

Melvin recruited over three hundred volunteer parents with preschool children from the community. The families were randomly assigned to three groups: (1) control group (parents received no intervention), (2) information group (parents received a special explanatory temperament profile letter and a packet of management appropriate for the child as rated by the parents), and (3) nurse intervention group (parents received personal intervention from a pediatric nurse). The questionnaires of temperament and behavior problems of the children were filled out by the parents. For group 3 the pediatric nurses utilized had considerable experience with assessment of child development and behavior, parenting skills, anticipatory guidance, and family counseling, and also interest in temperament. The nurses, in effect, acted as temperament counselors for the parents who needed guidance for their children with behavior problems (Melvin, 1995).

The project is into its second year and proceeding smoothly. The findings of these controlled groups promise to answer several important questions: Can parents utilize useful guidance temperament information and modify positively their functioning with children with difficulties? Can a trained nurse with a short series of sessions with parents provide them with effective guidance on their children's difficulties and behavior problems?

The final findings of Melvin's project will be awaited with great interest. By now our NYLS concepts of temperament and goodness of fit have been applied with parent guidance in many centers and in the individual practice of mental health professionals and educators.

This clinical experience has been objectively confirmed in the Kaiser Permanente program (see Chapter 13). Melvin's objective, sophisticated project will bear importantly on the evidence of parent guidance and the usefulness of experienced nurses as temperament counselors for parent guidance.

Sandra McClowry, R.N., Ph.D., associate professor of nursing at New York University, has been awarded a substantial grant from a private foundation, as part of a comprehensive school-based health center in an elementary inner-city school in New York. Since late 1994, parents of children in the school's kindergarten to fifth grade have been invited to take part in a temperament-based parenting program. The selective intervention lasts 10 weeks, during which time the parents are taught to recognize and appreciate the temperament of their children and then to develop effective management strategies. She evaluates the effectiveness of the program in several ways. Changes in the children's behavior are assessed through information from the teachers and parents at the beginning and end of the school year and before and after parental participation in the temperament-based intervention. Social competence of the children and parental distress are evaluated at the beginning and end of the school year. Academic data are collected and compared with data from another school in the same community that does not have a prevention center.

McClowry expects to complete the analysis of her data in the forthcoming year and publish it in one of the nursing journals. Her report should be significant, a pioneering study of the value of a temperament program in prevention of and early intervention in the behavior and academic problems in disadvantaged inner city school children.

In addition, McClowry and her coworkers (McClowry et al., 1994) reported the findings of an extensive and sophisticated study of the effects of child temperament, maternal characteristics, and family circumstances on the maladjustment of school-age children.

Finally, in June 1995, a leading nursing journal, the *Journal of Pediatric Nursing*, published a special issue of a series of research papers on the "Clinical Applications of Children's Temperament." Seven nurses from a variety of academic centers in the country contributed and have received funding for their research in the field of temperament. The topics of the articles include the influence of temperament on the parenting of infants, the manifestations of temperament in toddlers, a temperament intervention program for parents of preschool children, interviews for temperament-relative behavior in middle childhood, the influence of temperament in children with disabilities, the influence of temperament on the responses of children who are ill and/or hospitalized, and a study of the temperaments of infants with and without colic. Melvin and McClowry, the coeditors of this special issue, intended these articles "to entice nurses to learn more about temperament and to stimulate researchers and clinicians" (Melvin & McClowry, 1995, p. 140).

As we ourselves watch the burgeoning number and projects of nurses involved in research on and clinical applications of temperament, we label this phenomenon an exciting development.

18

TEMPERAMENT AND PSYCHOTHERAPY OF CHILDREN

Dr. Joan trained as a child psychiatrist through the New York University–Bellevue Medical Center residency and fellowship programs, was bright, was fully responsible for all her assignments, had interesting innovative ideas, and socialized easily and cooperatively with the staff.

When Joan graduated, in the 1970s, she indicated an interest in becoming a full-time staff psychiatrist at Bellevue Hospital. Our faculty were all pleased at her choice, and offered her an available position in my (S.C.) special pediatric psychiatric liaison clinic. "Liaison" meant close association with the general pediatric clinic, both geographically and functionally. I immediately arranged for her to be a responsible member of the clinic. Joan, with her talents and assets, easily and quickly became a valuable member of the staff. Beyond her routine responsibilities, which were done splendidly, she also made strong positive relationships with the pediatric staff, which regarded the liaison service as one of the pediatric specialty clinics.

Within a few years, a senior position in our clinic became available and I promptly promoted her. As I expected, Joan carried through her additional responsibili-

141

ties thoroughly and competently. After about 5 years and
after her maternity leave following the birth of her first
child, she told me she wanted to go into full-time private
practice and resign her clinic position. I was surprised
and disappointed, but it was her choice and she maintained friendly contact with the staff.

Although our paths crossed occasionally, we had not
had any opportunities for clinical discussions. I met her
by chance on the outside sidewalk of the hospital 10 years
later. We greeted each other and Joan burst out, "Stella,
I have to tell you about my case. For almost a year, I had
been intensively treating an 8-year-old boy with many behavioral problems without any success. And also I just
couldn't identify the dynamics of his symptoms. I thought
it must have been the parents' fault, but the parents and
the family were healthy, and I couldn't blame the parents
for the boy's problem. I was puzzled and frustrated, and
then suddenly I had an inspiration. This must be a boy
with difficult temperament, and a poorness of fit with the
parents' handling must be the cause of his behavioral difficulties. It was like a jigsaw puzzle with all the pieces
coming together in a clear pattern. I shifted my treatment
approach to a program of discussions of parent guidance,
with the principle of goodness of fit. As you have described this policy to us, I explained the nature of temperament, the normal but unusual behavior for a child with
difficult temperament, and that this required a different
but specific approach handling the boy's behavior. The
parents, who were intelligent and thoughtful, quickly understood the reasons for my advice. With a few discussions, the parents changed their approach, now there was
a goodness of fit, as you called it. Literally, the boy's difficulties melted, and in a month he was cured, and I dis-
charged him. I checked a 6-month follow-up, just last
week, and parents and boy are all doing very well." I
was delighted.

THE MYTH OF EARLY LIFE EXPERIENCE

Dr. Joan's story provides a wealth of lessons for the practice of psychotherapy for children. First and foremost, the diagnosis must be accurate; the same rule is true for treatment in all fields of medicine.

This rule seems obvious for child therapists, but it is perhaps the most treacherous one in the evaluation of a child's behavioral problem. The young organism is immature; its development from the beginning is the evolution of complex interweaving of many organic factors and life experiences.

In classical psychoanalytic theory and in popular thought, a child with a behavior problem does not have the same degree of complexity of behavioral dysfunctional development as does an adult, because of the interactional processes of a number of pathogenic factors and life experiences over time. The child psychiatrist, dealing with a briefer life span, has seemingly a relatively easy task in making a diagnosis. Presumably it is necessary to identify one of the primary traumas that in this short life span has caused this immature organism behavioral dysfunction.

In the past half century, many, and perhaps most, child therapists have opted for a primary cause—a pathogenic dysfunctional family with the outstanding culprit being the mother. Other factors may or may not be added as secondary influences, factors such as environmental stresses, conditioning, sociocultural issues, and attachment theory. With few exceptions, the favorite formulation, and even the secondary factors as well, have embraced the concept that the decisive period in the development of behavioral dysfunction is the early life years. "Traditionally, theories of psychological development, whatever their bias, have generally procured a linear predictable sequence from conception, birth or early childhood only" (Chess 1979, p. 109). As an example, a prominent child development researcher asserted, "I see our apparent inability to make empirical predictions about later personality from the early years as so much against good sense, common observation, and the thrust of all developmental theories that I can take it only as indictment of established paradigms and methods rather than as evidence of a developmental reality" (Bronson, 1974).

However, "good sense" and "common observation" have never been reliable criteria for the validity of scientific theory. The classic book by the Clarkes (1976) has much important data. In their volume, they have documented the findings of a widespread series of research studies of the effects of early life experience by a number of eminent workers that all lead to the emphatic conclusion: "The whole of development is important, not merely the early years. There is as yet no indication that a stage is clearly more formative than others; in the long-term all may be important" (Clarke and Clarke, 1976, p. 272).

The Clarkes' conclusions are echoed by a host of researchers and by our own NYLS findings (Chess, 1979). Unfortunately, the unproven thesis that a child's behavioral problem is caused by a dysfunctional family in the first few years of life is being only slowly reconsidered. This theory is the only one considered by many child therapists, to this day.

But now our NYLS findings, and the studies of others, have introduced the formulation that the temperament–environment maladaptation leading to a poorness of fit may create a behavioral dysfunction at any age period—infancy, preschool and school years, adolescence, and adulthood. As we have detailed in preceding chapters, this thesis and its implications have been strongly accepted by pediatricians, nurses, developmental psychologists, and educators.

WRONG DIAGNOSIS OF DIFFICULT TEMPERAMENT

In my consultative practice, many of the families were referred to me with the story that one of the children had suffered a behavioral problem and been diagnosed and treated for many months by a good child therapist without improvement. My strong impression, after I had done a careful history and play interview, was that the most frequent cause of the wrong diagnosis and treatment was inattention to the possibility of difficult temperament of the child and poorness of fit with the parents. Dr. Joan's mistaken diagnosis, in her account above, was a typical story. Fortunately, Dr. Joan was talented and had been actively introduced to the concept and implication of temperament in her Bellevue training. After a long period of unsuccessful treatment of the child, she reevaluated her diagnosis, recognized the error, corrected her diagnosis, and changed her treatment approach to parent guidance with a successful outcome within a few weeks.

Unfortunately, the cases referred to me after a long continued period of unsuccessful treatment had been by child therapists with no early causal awareness of temperament. Consequently, this possible factor had not been considered.

Child therapists faced with the diagnosis and treatment of a child with a behavioral problem are bound to go wrong if they are inattentive to the possibility of the presence of temperamental styles in the child that the parents have found incompatible with their own expectations. Recognizing that the parents' handling has resulted in a poorness of fit and suggesting alternates is not the same as blaming the parent (see Chapter 8). In such a case, the therapist can be easily seduced by the "evidence" and be convinced that this is a dysfunctional family. The behavioral temperamental characteristics may become evident in early childhood. Beyond that, the mother, who has been struggling with the difficulties of caregiving with such a child, does not realize that these behaviors are an expression of temperament. The problems of sleeping schedules; introduction of new foods, people, or places; toilet training; and the like all too often lead to self-blame as a poor mother with anxiety, guilt, and defensiveness.

The therapist misinterprets the mother's distress as the cause rather than the effect of the child's behavior.

EASE OF PARENT GUIDANCE

In Dr. Joan's case, fortunately the use of parent guidance required only a short series of discussions. The parents were intelligent and flexible. They understood the nature of the child's temperamental pattern and were able to correct their handling of the child from a poorness to a goodness of fit. In many other cases, parent guidance may require many sessions before parents grasp the concepts of temperament and slowly achieve goodness of fit; also, they may be relatively rigid in their ability to modify or change their caregiving practices (see Chapter 9). Psychotherapy for the child may be needed too; it is always a variable task—sometimes moving quickly, sometimes prolonged, sometimes in between.

OTHER TEMPERAMENT ATTRIBUTES FOR PSYCHOTHERAPY

The discussion above has focused on the temperament–environment relationship, with maladaptation in cases with difficult temperament. These are often the most dramatic cases, either for success or failure. But issues can come up with poorness of fit with other temperamental clusters. Slow-to-warm-up children may become shy, and anxious with new situations; very active children may become tense and behaviorally disturbed if not given the space and opportunities to use their motor activity adequately and constructively at home or at school; highly persistent youngsters may be frustrated by abrupt termination of their absorption in a time-demanding activity.

As a final caveat, the pendulum may swing too widely to the assumption that any child's behavioral problem must have a temperamental basis. In some cases, temperament is important. But there are many instances in which the causation of a child's disorder may have only a modest, minimal, or even negligible basis in temperament.

19

TEMPERAMENT AND PSYCHOTHERAPY OF ADOLESCENTS

When 13-year-old Virginia was brought to me (S.C.) for psychiatric evaluation, her problems were considerable, even though she did not have a major psychiatric disorder. She had many assets. She was of very superior intelligence, was well coordinated, had a wide range of interests, and, with her high persistence, became easily proficient at any skill that caught her fancy. Yet she had made no lasting friendships, and was constantly fighting with her two younger sisters and with her parents as well. They came to the conclusion that they and she needed help. Basically they believed themselves to be good parents, and their relationships with 11-year-old Susan and 9-year-old Vera bore this out.

The parents, Dr. and Mrs. Leonard, were themselves exceedingly intelligent and competent. Dr. Leonard, a biochemist, was in charge of a large division of a business concern. Mrs. Leonard had been a teacher before the birth of her children. In place of formal employment, she now devoted a great deal of time to parents' associations and volunteer church and community work. Ginny had been a wanted child who had been healthy, and her development had been normal and advanced.

Problems were reported to have started with the beginning of nursery school. Prior to that, although Ginny had been a colicky baby and as a toddler had had mammoth temper tantrums, both parents had dealt with these without considering them unusual parenting issues. Ginny had always had a difficult time adapting to new events, but this too had been handled appropriately by her parents, who introduced their advancing expectations gradually and respected her styles of slow accommodation.

In school, however, Ginny's social behavior was increasingly problematic. As she grew older, her tantrums continued. With her increasing size and sophisticated vocabulary, she alienated both teachers and classmates. At home, more and more she violated the family tone of reasonable discussions. Her parents had initially questioned the competence of her schools, but after two school changes, concluded that the fault lay in Ginny's own behavior.

As I reviewed my history from the parents, it became more and more clear that Ginny's style of behavior since infancy had fit the temperamental cluster that we have called "the difficult child." She had been biologically irregular from infancy on, withdrew from new situations and people, adapted very slowly, was more often in a negative than a positive mood, and showed her feelings with high intensity. To this cluster were added the temperamental traits of high persistence and high activity level. Although each of these qualities was entirely normal, in combination they were formidable. On those occasions when her desires coincided with those of her parents, teachers, or classmates, she was a great asset and a pleasure to be with. But when she grew older, her disagreements became louder and emphatic in expression, and the persistence and high intellectual quality of her arguments were burdensome. In school, such episodes brought classroom teaching to a halt, and other children, after one or two miserable adventures with her tongue lashings, preferred to keep her at a distance. Once each episode was behind her, Ginny would forget it and could not understand why other people held such unreasonable grudges against her. Hence, she would not agree that she had made any contribution to this growing distressing situation of everybody picking on her. The good fit that her parents had managed to maintain through Ginny's toddler and preschool period was fast eroding.

While it was clear that Ginny's temperamental qualities had been prominent in the creation and maintenance of her behavior disorder, it was equally clear that the constantly accelerating vicious cycle would not be able to be reversed simply by clarifying the temperamental component. The Leonards were quite accepting of the temperament description and ready to modify their approaches if desirable. They agreed that psychotherapy was also essential and became capable, objective, and intelligent colleagues in the therapeutic process that, we all agreed, would not show immediate success. The ultimate aim of psychotherapy would be for Ginny to gain self-knowledge and learn how to use this to be in control of her own behavior. During this process, it was also our aim to restore her own self-esteem, which had been fast eroding, and help her to develop a social intelligence in terms of gaining awareness of and respect for the behavioral styles of other individuals. Most particularly, Ginny needed to learn to be an observer of the social scene and learn the differing social expectations against which to judge the appropriateness of her own spontaneous reactions. Literally, up to then she seemed unaware that reducing a friend to tears was an unfriendly act, or that calling a teacher ignorant, even if true, was not appropriate in a classroom.

Most important, Ginny was highly motivated to change her life. True, she saw herself as the victim, the guardian of truth in a world of hypocrites, but basically she was deeply attached to her family, was capable of generous actions, and genuinely believed her parents to be a refuge when the world crashed down on her in so bewildering

a manner. Therapy was an irregular process. My meetings
with the Leonards enabled me, through their amazingly
objective descriptions of noteworthy episodes, to extend
Ginny's perceptions to the fuller picture. Gradually, it became possible to enlarge her own awareness by my persistence in asking for her own literal and blow-by-blow accounts. Finally, it became possible to take her own
accounts as a basis for examining the effect of her actions
on the needs and feelings of others. The focus was on
helping Ginny to learn to be effective in expressing her
ideas rather than antagonizing others. The first four times
when I suggested a modification of Ginny's contentious
manner of presenting an idea at school, she blew up at
me and treated me to samples of her typical problem behavior. I watched quietly until the smoke cleared. Then
I told her I was impressed by the thoughtfulness of her
comment. If others agreed, or modified or criticized her
idea, that didn't mean that they were her enemy. Quite
the contrary, such responses indicated that her idea had
stimulated thought. This might result in agreement, in
modification, or in disagreement. It might even expand
the essence of her idea. So, I told her, when you just made
that interesting comment to me, I respected your thinking
and wanted you to learn to join the discussion with respect for your classmates' opinions. Only if you respect
and really listen to what they say, will they be ready to
do the same for you. Finally, on the fourth occasion, she
really began to listen to my comments. With that, we were
on the homestretch. She agreed that she would, in fact,
be more competent if she could guide her actions by
her aims.

The real breakthrough occurred when Ginny phoned
me one day before her next appointment. She said she
was all steamed up about an injustice in school and that
she knew she would create a commotion after which she
would lose the possibility of being heard. She did agree
that my advice would be more helpful if she obtained a
larger picture of the situation from her parents, and it did

turn out that Ginny was right about the current injustice. But, she had been ignored in an atmosphere of rightful annoyance with her over the recent campaigns she had waged over rather insignificant slights. I arranged to have a discussion with Ginny and her parents early the next morning before school. In this atmosphere in which three adults were willing to rearrange their schedules because they found her needs so important, Ginny was able to make her first giant step toward self-knowledge. The next morning she carefully rehearsed the presentation she planned to make, with her parents suggesting useful touches. She was also fortunate that, overnight, the school authorities had also realized that Ginny, although she had cried wolf very often, this time had a genuine grievance. She was surprised at the school's attitude, they were surprised at Ginny's ability to state her position in a reasonable manner, and a new and positive dynamic of behavior was now initiated.

Let me not give the impression that the course of further therapy was a smooth, benign cycle. Ginny continued to adapt slowly, saw the negative aspects of a new situation or person automatically, and familiarity was a necessary precursor for positive interactions. She continued to be highly intense, highly persistent, and in need of a great deal of physical activity. But more and more these temperamental qualities were applied productively, and there were more expressions of zestful enjoyment than of explosive destructive episodes. And, as she approached young adulthood, she used her home support system more and more often to clarify issues before acting. At her own desire and with her parents' approval, for a period of several years, Ginny would arrange appointments with me during college vacations, during which she would review events, both positive and negative, to gain more objectivity. More often than not, she had found her own solutions. Yearly Christmas cards brought up to date the picture of a successful career in the areas of her own choosing. By then her predominantly positive intensity showed her bubbling, spirited expressions in her periods of absorbed and pleasurable involvement in her interests.

THE NEW STRESSES OF ADOLESCENCE

Each succeeding developmental period makes new demands on the growing child, the adolescent, and the adult. In our society, adolescence is frequently labeled as an especially stressful period. For example, adolescence is often viewed as "a period of extraordinary change, multiple conflicts, and masked societal demands on the individual" (Fishman, 1982, p.39). This formulation may confirm the story of Ginny's development.

In Ginny's case, in adolescence she was faced with the stress of new and more demanding social expectations. Other adolescents may have to struggle and cope with other stresses: sexual development about which they are ambivalent or in conflict, seduction of experimentation with drugs or alcohol, conflict with inflexible parents. However, if Ginny had traits of easy and less persistent temperament, her childhood development undoubtedly would have been easy and smooth, and she would have coped in adolescence with the new social and academic demands with mild or even minimal stress.

THE MYTH OF NORMAL ADOLESCENT TURMOIL

Traditionally, both in popular and professional writings, adolescence has been viewed as a normal period of marked emotional upheaval and turmoil arising from rapid physical changes, the onset of adult sexuality, and the expectations for increased responsibility within the family combined with beginnings of autonomy in functioning. This view was formulated vividly by G. Stanley Hall in his classic volume on adolescence in 1904: "The teens are emotionally unstable and pathetic. It is a natural impulse to experience hot and proverbial psychic states" (Hall, 1904, vol. 11, p.74). This concept was elaborated by influential psychoanalysts, which even led to the assertion that adolescence was inevitable as a period of emotional ability and instability, in which the upholding of a steady equilibrium would itself be abnormal (Blos, 1979; Eissler, 1958; A. Freud, 1958; Erikson, 1959). The psychoanalytic rationalization for this concept of normal adolescent turmoil was well summarized: "The functions of ego and superego are severely strained. Instinctual impulses disrupt the homeostatic arrangements achieved during latency, and inner turmoil results. . . . Unresolved preoedipal or oedipal conflicts are revived, the repression characteristic of latency is no longer sufficient to restore a psychological equilibrium" (Offer & Offer, 1975, p. 161).

These psychoanalytic formulations have been derived primarily from data obtained from adolescent or adult patients suffering from one of another psychopathologic syndrome. Indeed, the studies of unsolicited groups do provide a different picture of this developmental stage. Coleman's (1978) survey of the literature found that the large-scale empirical studies have concluded that "In light of empirical investigation, the full-blown storm and stress syndrome of adolescence appears to be relatively insubstantial." Rutter's (1979) comprehensive and systematic review of the pertinent literature came to a similar judgment. "It is also evident that normal adolescence is not characterized by storm, stress, and disturbance" (Rutter, 1979, p. 86).

These respected judgments of the myth of adolescent turmoil are further confirmed by a careful study of Offer and Offer (1975) and the findings of our own NYLS (Chess & Thomas, 1984). We have followed our subjects from childhood to adult life and have grouped them as follows during their adolescent period: (1) smooth, expansive adolescence; (2) turbulent but healthy adolescence; (3) childhood disorder and mastery in adolescence; (4) poorness of fit in adolescence. The reasons for the evolution of the adolescent pattern varied widely in the subjects, but in most cases temperament issues contributed a modest to a marked influence. In the case of Ginny, detailed above, her temperamental traits dictated a turbulent but healthy adolescence.

THE "GENERATION GAP"

Another popular idea, that of the generation gap between parents and their adolescent children, did not impress Rutter, the Offers, or ourselves.

We have emphasized a critique of the popular ideas of normal adolescent turmoil and the ubiquitous generation gap in theory and treatment. To embrace these concepts emphasizes anew the fallacy of applying any unidimensional linear theoretical model to this or any other life span theory.

20

TEMPERAMENT AND PSYCHOTHERAPY OF ADULTS

Mr. and Mrs. Stewart, a young couple with severe marital problems, came to me for consultation. They had explosive quarrels over even simple disagreements, which had been getting worse over their 10 years of marriage. They were very concerned about their two children, 8 and 6 years old. They were devoted to both children, who were delightful youngsters. Both parents had begun to notice that during the past years, when they quarreled, the children would get upset, cry, and beg them to stop these fights. The parents justifiably feared that their quarrels were becoming harmful to the children. They promised them they would stop these blowups, but were not able to do so. But the Stewarts were also puzzled. They had congenial agreements over major issues—politics, finances, method of handling the children, ethical standards, and so on. The fights were not over such issues, but limited only to simple routine matters. They had consulted a good marital counselor, but the advice, which seemed reasonable, had not helped.

The Stewarts had met in college, were quickly attracted to each other, and found their interests and values compatible. Even then they did have quarrels over minor disagree-

157

ments, but these lasted only a few minutes, and appeared unimportant. Soon after graduation they were married. They launched their different professional careers, at which both succeeded, and started a basically harmonious marriage and a promising family with healthy children. Yet, over the years, their marriage headed for disaster and serious distress for the children.

I pressed the husband and wife for the possible cause of their bitter friction. Did one or both have competitive or jealous feelings over the other's career? Did they have sexual problems? Was one or more of their in-laws interfering in their marriage in some provocative or destructive manner? To their knowledge, was one or the other or both involved in extramarital affairs? For all these questions, both answered no.

I took the next tack. I asked the Stewarts to describe the details of their last quarrel, only 4 days ago. The wife started. Their car was 3 years old, and she wanted to turn the car in for a new one. The husband responded that the car was in good shape and reliable and certainly they didn't need a new car; maybe in a year or two. The wife replied with anger that he knew she worried lest the car break down when she was driving; she would be reassured with a new car. "We have plenty of money, don't be a skinflint." With that, the husband shouted, "You know I'm never stingy. And you're being anxious over an unreasonable worry. You can always call the AAA if the car breaks down." The wife shrieked, "I know you would replace anything that might worry you, like the lawn mower. You're entirely unreasonable with me." They became engrossed in the quarrel and acted out a typical incident before me, escalating their charges and blaming each other, and were almost ready to throw something at each other. I calmed them down, gave them a breathing spell. I suspected that the culprit might be their emotional intensity. I said nothing, but arranged another appointment for seeing each separately.

In his appointment, I asked Mr. Stewart if He could remember whether when he was a child he had had tantrums when he was frustrated. He answered quickly, "I certainly did, but my mother or father just waited patiently, didn't give in to me, and finally my tantrum ended. I knew my parents would win, and, after all, with most things I really wanted, they were quite reasonable. So I went on my cheerful way." I asked the next question, "When you played baseball and the umpire called a decision you thought was unfair, did you get excited?" He promptly answered, "I did, I shouted and screamed, but I knew it wouldn't help, so I would go on with the game." I asked a final question, "If you got a big promotion, how excited would you get?" "No question," he said, "I'd feel at the top of the world and arrange a celebration. It was funny. When some of my friends would get a successful achievement, they were pleased, but just acted quietly. They must be happy, but why didn't they get excited, the way I did? It puzzled me." I thanked him, and said I would arrange another joint appointment for both of them. The husband was openly upset, having expected an immediate solution.

In the meeting alone with Mrs. Stewart, my questions and her answers were almost an identical replay of the discussion with her husband. As to tantrums when she was a child, she certainly had them. Her parents handled them by waiting her out. She lost, but finally went along cheerfully. As to her social group as a teenager, if the group decided to go on a trip and she objected, she was vigorous in her disagreement, but the others usually refused to change the plan. "I did get very upset, but I had to control myself quickly, otherwise I would be left without friends." As to her special commendations and promotions, "I sure got excited, and brought home a bottle of champagne to celebrate with my husband. He was just as excited for me and we had a great time, the children too. Somehow my friends don't get as exuberant when something good happens with them. I know they are pleased, but you can't tell it, and that puzzles me." I thanked her and said I would arrange another joint appointment for both of them. She was taken aback and almost cried, "I had my hopes pinned on your advice and you haven't told me anything."

Both husband and wife came to the next appointment promptly. They were both obviously very tense. I suspected that, on the one hand, they hoped I would give them a magical solution. On the other hand, they were afraid I would give them a hopeless judgment.

I explained that I would give advice, but it would be useful only if they understood its basis. "I do have an explanation for you, but it's not magic. Do you know anything about the psychological concept called temperament?" They shook their heads, said "Vaguely," and looked bewildered. I then went into a detailed discussion of the nature of temperament, the research findings in the field, and the concept of goodness of fit. Then I told them that both of them had high intensity of mood expression, involving both positive and negative feelings. That is why they enjoy themselves so thoroughly with each other, their children, and their friends. But, unfortunately, their intensity is also expressed with negative feelings. Thus they each become angry and bitter when they are frustrated over even a minor disagreement, and their anger escalates, with reinforcement from each other, to a serious blowup. This was a style of behavior and did not indicate actual incompatibility.

Gradually the Stewarts began to understand what I had explained. Both blurted out, "But what can we do? Are you saying we can't change our temperament?" With that, I went into a comprehensive program of behavioral guidance. I summarized the basic principles. They both had so many positive attributes; they loved each other and their children deeply. Their positive emotional responses could be exuberant and even extravagant without creating problems. But their negative emotional reactions could wreck their family and endanger the future of their children. They were both adults, normal and intelligent, and were motivated to save their family. Each had to determine that if the other had a disagreement and became angry, both must recognize the anger as a danger signal and immediately determine to find a positive compromise or other solution. If necessary, they should go into different rooms till they were calm. Remember the aim: Express the disagreement but not the anger. The aim is to find a solution, not to win. If helpful, they should postpone a final agreement to a later time. I also suggested that they sit down with the two children and explain that they had found an answer to their fights. They wouldn't disappear overnight but would diminish. "You can stop worrying about us; we love each other and we love you."

I concluded the session by reviewing once again my explanation and advice, and made another joint appointment for the next week.

The Stewarts came in at the next appointed time and looked very unhappy. "What happened?" They both burst out, "We discussed your advice, it made sense. And then with the next disagreement, 3 days later, we went into a wingding fight, not better at all. We are just failures. What's the use!" I laughed, "You've been fighting for 10 years, and in one week you expected to change completely? Now, tell me the detail of this blowup." Both chimed in, describing the occurrence of a minor problem; they disagreed, got angry, and went into the familiar sequence. I thought for a moment, and then proposed a simple solution: "You have a quota of two shouts each, no more. I am sure that that is even more than you permit yourself at work." They were chagrined and wondered why they could not have thought of such a simple rule themselves. I explained, "The reason is simple but profound. Once you become angry, you can no longer think. Remember the rule, don't express anger but use your passion for finding a solution. Underneath you know that your positive relationship is more important than an individual issue. People can agree to disagree, neither *must* win."

The Stewarts came in for their next appointment, this time looking triumphant. "What happened?" They rushed in with a new story. They had a disagreement 2 days ago, started to attack each other, and suddenly stopped. "But we knew we had to stop this and find a solution. We waited a moment, then began to discuss how we could solve this problem. It took a few minutes and we found the answers on which we both agreed. We whooped and embraced each other." I said to them, "I congratulate you. You have solved a problem in 2 weeks that has bedeviled you for 10 years, but it isn't that simple. The new behavior is not yet an established habit." We planned other appointments scheduled at increasingly longer intervals, as needed.

They came in for their next appointment a month later and beamed at me. "We have an A report. We've had only one fight, over some silly business. We were tired and worried over our son who was ill. We forgot our rule, the only time." I said, "You and all of us can't be perfect. But I'm sure you have really licked this problem." They added, "You know, that rule—'don't show anger, look for a solution'—has helped us in both our jobs. We work better, and our colleagues are more friendly than they used to be." They said goodbye, and their yearly Christmas card says, "We're fine, thanks."

I have seen other cases of severe marital problems that stemmed from temperamentally driven behavior. A number of couples had to struggle for many weeks or months before reaching a successful conclusion. A few, sadly, just failed. Their pathological entanglements were so deep that the only solution was divorce.

Beyond the issue of a marital conflict, should the basic cause of a severe behavior disorder be a temperament–environment maladaptation, a poorness of fit, then the guidance and counseling strategy can be the preeminent method of therapy. Guidance may be dramatically and quickly successful, or may require lengthy discussion, or may fail. These comments are true for children and adolescents as well as for adults.

A basic caveat must be remembered, whether for children, adolescents, or adults: Not all behavior disorders are created by a temperament–environment maladaptation. In some cases, a disorder such as schizophrenia, autism, manic-depressive illness, and others bear no causal relationship to temperament. In other conditions, such as brain damage, the influence of temperament may provide a secondary factor including the course of the disorder. In the latter case, temperament guidance may be desirable even if of only modest usefulness. It is always the clinician's judgment to assess, in any individual case, whether and how much temperament guidance should be employed.

THE OUTLOOK OF TEMPERAMENT IN ADULT PSYCHOTHERAPY

As has been detailed in previous chapters, the realization of the functional importance of temperament in research and practical programs for children has been expanded vigorously by mental health professionals and others over the years. By contrast, little attention has been paid to temperament theory and practice as they pertain to adults. But, as indicated in the case vignettes of the Stewarts above, the use of temperament guidance prognosis or temperament-based advice by individual practitioners is an important issue.

It is in fact much easier to identify the characteristics of temperament, and their definition and rating, in children than in adults. The combination of the characteristics and their interaction with other various aspects of a child's behavioral patterns, such as motivation, social cognition, and self-esteem, are relatively simple in the immature organism. In the mature adult whose various characteris-

tics, such as motivation and social cognition, have become much more complex in the decades of development, these functioning patterns are also influenced by
factors such as the growth of the brain and the elaboration
of language and learning. The host of life experiences en-
countered from infancy to adult life has also shaped the
complexity of the adult's behavioral patterns. Nevertheless, by obtaining descriptions of behavior in a number of
situations, it is not difficult to determine whether the
adult is shy or gregarious, mild mannered or intense, persistent or yielding, physically active or sedentary, among
other temperamental characteristics that may play a part
in problems.

There is one central barrier to the utilization of temperament theory. Most qualified psychotherapists have been
trained and then have practiced according to psychoanalytic–psychodynamic concepts and methods of treatment. It is always difficult, in any field, for a professional
who has been taught within a specific ideational system,
has accepted its logic, and has based a career of psychotherapy, teaching, and perhaps research on this theoretical structure to welcome alternative approaches. Accepting a new ideational system, with implications of
radical change in the professional's thinking and functioning, is indeed an enormous demand. The new system,
based on an examination of temperament–environment
maladaptation, poorness of fit, and guidance and documented by objective and scientific data using concepts
and practice that are relatively simple to comprehend,
may markedly reduce the time, money, and suffering for
many cases and offer programs of prevention and early
intervention of treatment. Nevertheless, it can be very
painful to abandon an established and secure ideational
professional life course of theory and practice.

Over the past 25 years, I (S.C.) have been invited to
present lectures and discussions on temperament at special seminars at medical centers and organizations both
nationally and internationally. Uniformly, my experi-

ences with these presentations have been positive. The audience listens with interest, and at the end of my lecture asks many questions that indicate they have grasped the essential ideas I have presented. However, very rarely does a member of the audience come up to me or write to me and say, "You have made temperament meaningful, interesting, and important. Could you suggest how I could be trained regarding temperament, so I could change my research and my practice?"

The vignette about Dr. Joan at the beginning of Chapter 18 is instructive. Joan had been an active, full-time, responsible member of my child psychiatry liaison clinic at Bellevue. She had contributed much at our frequent case conferences, at which a staff member presented an account of a problem and then described all the possible causes of the disorder: family history, social stresses, intellectual level, school and social history, developmental history, motivations and goals, medical history, and temperament. The child was first interviewed, and then the staff members discussed their important findings, and dynamics of the reasons for the child's symptoms, made a diagnosis, and finally decided the proper course of treatment.

The case discussion always included an evaluation of the child's temperament. If it was of major importance, the treatment plan would be based largely on the techniques of analysis of the poorness of fit and parent guidance.

Joan attended these case conferences for 5 years, and always actively participated in discussing the dynamics and diagnoses of the cases. Yet, despite her experience at the clinic, she missed the diagnosis of difficult temperament as the major issue for a patient in her private practice for almost a year. She eventually recognized the correct diagnosis and was able to shift expertly to a temperament treatment approach, and her success required only a few weeks.

The reason for the delay in her diagnosis appears to be
a puzzle, but I can suggest an answer. Dr. Joan's training
in both her general and child psychiatry curriculum at
Bellevue included the psychotherapeutic management of
a number of individual cases outside the liaison clinic.
Her psychodynamic approach to the families of children,
adolescents, and adults was supervised by experienced
faculty members of the Bellevue/NYU staff. The majority
of her supervisors were committed, as in other training
centers, to the psychodynamic–psychoanalytic thesis that
the diagnosis and treatment of a behavior disorder with
a psychological basis are based on its causation by a dysfunctional family in the early childhood years. Dr. Joan
had been influenced by this theory, and the additional
important, but not exclusive, formulation of temperament–environment maladaptation and poorness of fit had
been learned but not fully absorbed outside of her work
at the child psychiatry liaison clinic. In her own clinical
practice, I can only postulate that she relied basically on
the specific psychodynamic diagnostic and treatment
principles that she had learned under formal supervision.
When faced with a case in which her analytic-style treatment was unsuccessful, she concluded that, at least in
that case, her psychodynamic approach was failing. Only
then was she free to think of the alternative temperament
approach she had also learned; she switched to this treatment approach and succeeded dramatically. Unfortunately, many therapists cling rigidly to their psychodynamic concepts, and if they fail in some cases, explain
their failure by rationalizations, usually in terms of possible sabotage by the child's mother based on unconscious
reasons from her own traumatic past—a standard psychoanalytic explanation.

AN OPTIMISTIC VIEW FOR THE FUTURE

A number of separate recent and current incidents that
have come to our attention led us to an optimistic view

of the coming years. There is a growing number of good therapists who are using temperament issues in their practice. The expansion of parent education (see Chapter 12) and the success of the Kaiser Permanente Temperament Program have oriented therapists to the importance of temperament issues in diagnosis and treatment.

These advances are not spectacular but incremental. The trend is clearly toward the eventual social recognition of the value of temperament issues as they apply to clinical practice.

21

TEMPERAMENT AND THE HANDICAPPED CHILD

Barbara, a 10-year-old, suffered from a hearing handicap from birth. During Barbara's gestation, her mother had contracted a mild case of rubella. Unfortunately, the virus was transmitted to the unborn child and produced serious defects to her developing organs.

Barbara was born with a severe hearing loss in one ear and a moderately severe loss in the other. Her intelligence was above average, and she was physically attractive. As to her temperament, she was always a difficult child, with intense negative reactions to any new situation and with slow adaptation. With the combination of her hearing problem and difficult temperament, she had periods of loud fussing and occasional tantrums at home, nursery school, and the early grade years in school. Once adapted to the situation, she was a pleasant, cooperative child. Fortunately, her parents and teachers understood the meaning of her periods of frustration and occasional brief outbursts and waited them out patiently.

Because of the severity of her hearing handicap, Barbara was placed, from the first grade, into a school for the deaf. With her high intelligence and sensitive, supportive teachers she adapted successfully and mastered her school work. In a total communication curriculum she learned lip reading and also American sign language.

Then, in her fifth grade, the teacher offered her mother the option for Barbara to move to a mainstream regular school and class. Instruction in words would make high demands on Barbara's oral skills, but the school did have a resource teacher for deaf children. Her mother was troubled over the decision. Mainstreaming gives the opportunity for a better education and social exposure to the non-deaf world, giving wider latitude for later educational choices. Barbara could cope with a more demanding curriculum in a regular school with her good intelligence. But could she master behaviorally all the new situations in such a change—a new building, new classmates, new teacher, and new type of curriculum—with her difficult temperament? Beyond that, her mother had checked and discovered that Barbara would have to take a special bus to and from school. The bus driver had an irritable personality and strict rules of order to maintain his concentration on driving.

With this dilemma, the mother consulted me (S.C.). I had previously done a consultation with her parents when Barbara had had difficulties as a preschooler. The clinical evaluation revealed that her problems were due to a rather extreme difficult temperament and a poorness of fit with the parents' inappropriate demands and expectations from her. I had explained the issue to them and offered ongoing guidance. Only a few sessions were required. The parents understood the nature of Barbara's temperament and changed their attitudes and handling to produce a goodness of fit. Barbara then developed with only minor problems, as indicated above. But with her difficult temperament, could she now cope with all the series of simultaneous new changes necessitated by a transfer to a general school?

The mother thoughtfully posed the details of the pro and con reasons for mainstreaming. After careful consideration, I felt strongly that Barbara, with her difficult temperament, could not successfully cope with all the changes to a new, strange general school. The stress and frustrations in the new school, or with the bus driver, would undoubtedly trigger many outbursts, and she would likely be unable to benefit academically and socially from the potential value of mainstreaming. The outcome could very well become a disaster. I advised the mother to make the choice of keeping Barbara familiar and adjusted at her school for the deaf. The mother was very relieved at my judgment; both parents agreed. Barbara, who had participated in this consideration, also wished to remain in her current school. She went successfully through the succeeding school years, including the high school years. The transition to a high school for the deaf was simple, because her classmates came along with her, and the school was situated in the same building as her grade school.

If Barbara's temperament had been easy and persistent, rather than difficult, with positive adaptation to the new, the story would have been different. Mainstreaming then would have been possible.

THE DRAMATIC STORY OF A DEAF PERSON

The story of Kate, in contrast Barbara's, is the dramatic achievement in life that is possible by a deaf young woman with a combination of intelligence, temperamental traits, high motivation, and many supportive individuals. The achievement was dramatic, but even with these assets, her successes did not come easily; quite the contrary.

Kate started in life as perfectly normal, with high intelligence and a supportive family. At age 9 years, she began to lose her hearing. The reason was completely obscure, and no treatment was possible. Her hearing worsened year by year, but she was able to master her academic demands through high school. She learned lip reading on her own, was determined to conceal her handicap and had no desire to transfer to a school for the deaf. She explained, "Usually I was seated in the front of the classroom because I was short and because my name was at the beginning of the alphabet. That was lucky!" Beyond that, her easy and persistent temperament served her well with her goals. She went to a good college, was determined to go into medicine, and went through her courses with excellent grades. Her classes were small, and she was able to sit at the front. She was completely frustrated in a course on the history of American art. The professor lectured every week for 3 hours in the dark showing slides. Without the possibility of lip reading in the dark, she couldn't understand what the professor said, and she had to drop the course and others like it.

She was accepted to medical school, but when she started she couldn't easily get a seat in the front of the room. One of her classmates noticed Kate's difficulty in getting a front seat as well as her mild speech defect and asked her about it. She told him her problem, which she had always kept a secret from everyone else. He promised to save her a seat every day in the front of the room and also take verbatim notes. "I sat next to him for 2 years, and if I missed something the lecturer said, I would glance at his notes. That really saved me."

Her medical school laboratory and clinical assignments with patients were usually one-to-one tasks, and Kate's lipreading served her successfully with these. She couldn't participate in the operating room, though, because all the students, residents, and attending surgeons were masked, and she was lost without lipreading. She confessed her problem to the surgical resident, who was sympathetic and covered any required operating room procedure.

At graduation Kate received her M.D. degree. She then enrolled for her general internship at a good hospital. The faculty quickly detected her hearing problem. Here the chief of medicine tried to persuade her to switch to a pa-thology internship, but she refused to do that as she wanted to work with live patients. Kate was put on probation for several months until the chief of medicine was satisfied that she could function at a high level and ensured that in her training responsibilities no patient would be harmed by her hearing impairment. I'm sure that some bright medical chiefs at hospitals would have forced Kate to resign medicine because they couldn't understand how a deaf doctor could take care of patients. However, this chief was respectful of her struggles and determination.

Kate did her service and teaching assignments successfully, and graduated after a year. She found she could work effectively with patients face-to-face with her lipreading and residual hearing but was closed out of most fields in which lipreading was not adequate in fulfilling responsibilities. She was accepted at an excellent psychiatric training hospital. Her staff was aware of her impairment and respected her achievements in spite of her handicap, and it was not an issue. Kate went through her 3-year residency without any serious problem, but she was always under stress. One circumstance or another inevitably came up in which her handicap interfered with her maximum talents, though her functioning was always adequate. At the completion of her residency, Kate received a staff position at an excellent clinic and did her job with a high level of patient service.

This detailed vignette of Kate's life illustrates how a handicapped person, whether deaf or with any other limitations, faces many stresses, problems, and frustrations in personal, academic, and vocational development. Kate was able to surmount these unending challenges and difficulties because of her talents and supportive family and colleagues. Beyond these favorable assets, her temperament as an easy, pleasant person, adaptable to frustrations and persistence, was crucial. If she had had a difficult temperament, as Barbara had, Kate could not have been able to master an academic and professional career and a diversified social life.

The importance of temperament in handicapped children became clear in my study of the special congenital rubella sample. A rubella epidemic in 1964 caused the infection of a large number of pregnant women in New York. The parents, themselves, did not have after effects from this apparently innocuous illness. Unfortunately, as with Barbara, the rubella virus had been transmitted from the mothers' blood through the placenta to the unborn children. Since the fetus gave nourishment the virus multiplied and interfered with the organs developing after the time of infection. Thus the timing of the maternal rubella determined which organs of the developing fetus would be damaged. After birth, children were found to have a variety of defects—hearing, visual, cardiac, cerebral functioning, and intelligence. The defects varied from mild to severe and from single to multiple ones. A multidisciplinary Rubella Defect Evaluation Project was established in the pediatrics department of NYU Medical Center. Its aim was to examine the clinical manifestations of the disease and to develop appropriate management techniques. In conjunction with this project, one of us (S.C.) and colleagues undertook a behavioral study, supported by the Federal Children's Bureau, to determine the psychological and psychiatric sequel of congenital rubella. This project, with a comprehensive study of the 243 cases, identified a number of significant findings (Chess, Korn, & Fernandez, 1971). An attempt to summarize the issues of the many types of handicaps in these congenital rubella children is beyond the scope of this volume. As indicated above, the importance of temperament in handicapped children will be summarized.

OVERVIEW OF TEMPERAMENT AND
THE HANDICAPPED CHILD

The temperamentally easy handicapped child is most likely to have positive experiences and, hence, positive

attitudes. The child's manner puts adults at ease: Having
the reassurance that the child will welcome their presence, adults dealing with deaf children, will more freely
and patiently repeat words, add pantomine for the deaf
child, and ask the youngster to repeat or write or panto-
mime what they failed to comprehend. Knowing that it
will be either accepted or refused in a pleasant manner,
adults are more likely to guide the visually handicapped
child in a matter-of-fact fashion or offer aid to the motorically disabled youngster. Thus, the easy child carries a
degree of invulnerability to hurt or discouragement—limited of course by the extent, kind, and number of handicaps. This is a child who is less likely to be taunted and
teased by other children and more likely to receive their
patience, welcome, and inclusion in activities.

The difficult handicapped child is at greatest risk for
evoking aversion in others. These children are more often
in a bad than a good mood, and they show their feelings—
often negative—in an intense way. New situations, people, and routines evoke withdrawal and protest, and adaptation takes a long time. Sleep, hunger, and elimination
patterns are irregular, and this further complicates the
smooth flow of routine functioning. When stresses occur,
stormy interactions are all too likely.

The slow-to-warm-up handicapped child also has a degree of vulnerability to psychological stress. Such children are exceedingly shy. With each new task, place, person, or event they have an initial withdrawal reaction.
Adaptation is slow, and during this gradual warming up
they find that groupings of other children have formed
that shut them out. The teacher may also interpret the
initial lack of involvement to mean dullness. Such children's temperament includes predominance of negative
mood of a mild or moderate intensity. Thus these children look deadpan or sulky, and when overlooked by others they see further confirmation of their belief that they
are unwanted. They may ascribe this rejection to their

handicap, when it may in fact be due to their manner of behavior.

Other individual temperamental attributes may also have a positive or negative effect on the psychological consequences of the handicap. Highly active children may create danger for themselves or others, thus evoking many limitations and prohibitions against which they rebel. Motorically quiet children may be seen as lethargic and intellectually slow, when this is in fact not the case. On the other hand, highly active children may be valued as athletes or errand runners, giving a positive psychologic flavor to their self-image. Quiet children's "goodness" may bring praise and a further feeling of being desirable. High persistence in tasks is praiseworthy, and the accomplishment this often brings is its own reward. On the other hand, if a child is engaged in a dangerous, disruptive, or unscheduled task, high persistence will bring censure, while low persistence will make it easy for the teacher to persuade the child to shift in another direction. In any of these cases, the attitude of the adult toward the temperamental expression of the child will influence the development of a positive or negative psychological set.

The lack of experience that these handicapped children have in many of the everyday social norms constitutes a real problem, a type of experiential deprivation. In order to learn the norms, not only of one's culture but also of one's subgroup, direct experience is indispensable. The handicapped child is often restrained in mobility, and this further hampers experiential opportunities. Handicapped children, especially deaf ones, are often considered emotionally immature and dependent.

Peers are essential to the handicapped child. Every child needs to feel accepted, a part of the group; if the child isn't, his or her self-esteem will necessarily suffer. For the handicapped child, association with peers is easiest in early childhood. The child who has difficulties in communication is not left out at the toddler stage, because communication in play takes place more through gestures and actions than through verbal exchanges. Verbalization at this developmental stage consists mostly of monologues with no response expected from the playmate. In middle childhood peer acceptance starts to be more difficult. If children attend a special school, it will probably be located at a considerable distance from where they live, thus depriving them of contact with neighborhood children. Thus these children have already become outsiders by virtue of attending a special school.

When the child reaches adolescence, participation and integration with peers become even more difficult. This happens at the time when the need for belonging to a group is very important. Many of the 14- and 15-year-olds in our study report how hurt they feel when neighborhood youngsters call them "retarded" or exclude them because they have difficulty in oral communication. The feeling of exclusion becomes acute at adolescence. The combination of being ostracized and the child's growing awareness of being different often precipitates a crisis, with the children blaming their parents or themselves for being handicapped. Parents feel very distressed by their child's lack of friends. They remember how important it was for them at this age to have friends. Some children who used to go outside and play with neighborhood youngsters when they were younger now refuse to go out, and parents report that neighborhood children who used to visit stop doing so as their child enters adolescence. Other parents tell us about their child's awareness of being included on the team only when no one else is available. Often the only friend the handicapped child has is someone who is also rejected by the other kids, the boy who cannot fight back and is beaten up all the time or a girl who is unpopular.

It is common for handicapped adolescents to engage in a lot of solitary activities: They shoot baskets by themselves, they swim, they read. They also often complain of being bored and lonely. A handicapped child needs to participate in planned activities; parents cannot rely on chance and casual meetings for such a child to make friends. The child will have to participate in extracurricular activities fundamentally for their social rather than their educational value. Being with other children in these activities will be very important in making friends, as well as in learning acceptable social behavior.

Some parents of handicapped children are very resourceful in finding activities in the community in which the child can participate. But even after parents have located them, they often find it difficult for their children to be accepted into a swimming class or a pottery class, although verbal communication, sight, and motor skills are not an essential element in these activities. Most parents do not know what resources are available within their community or their legal rights regarding their children's full participation. There is no central agency to direct them to the right recreational or educational facility, they often depend on teachers for advice.

We have found that the higher the social class of the parents of the handicapped child, the better the child's chances of participating in activities and meeting other children. The parents' neighborhood will determine the extracurricular resources available to the handicapped child. When facilities are not readily available or easily located, chances are that the handicapped child will spend most of the time after school with nothing to do.

Parents play a very important role: When children feel rejected by the outside world, the blow will not be so hard if they can retreat to a loving and warm family. Fortified by the way the family feels about them, they may later on feel strong enough again to face the outside world.

Within the family, sibs can become very important allies; their friends are often the first friends the handicapped child will know. A sib's willingness to include the handicapped sister or brother in the group is very important. Sibs often help the child with homework and can also be extremely helpful in communication. For example, we have found that quite often when deaf children have very few oral skills, the sibs learn sign language, often before and better than the parents. They often act as interpreter in the handicapped child's exchanges with relatives and friends.

We have all heard talk of a deaf, blind, or cerebral palsy subculture. As handicapped children grow, they become more aware of how different they are from the rest of society; there will be a growing tendency to spend time with people who have similar problems. This tendency is often a response to the prejudice and discomfort of nonhandicapped people in the presence of the handicapped. Thus social mainstreaming of a handicapped youngster can be even more difficult than educational mainstreaming (Chess et al., 1971).

SUMMATION

Temperament is only one of a number of functional variables (Barbara vs. Kate) that have special significance for the handicapped child's adaptive level at various developmental stages. The influence of specific temperamental attributes may be highly important with certain handicapped children and their supportive advantages, and at certain developmental stages, and of relatively minor significance in other cases and situations. No prior judgment can be made, and it is the clinician's task to evaluate the relative contribution of all the possible functional variables to the dynamics of a developmental course.

Once this task has been accomplished, the clinician can then proceed to a course of parent and teacher guidance to spell out those modifications of the stresses of the child required to achieve the goodness of fit that may promise a favorable development in the handicapped child (Chess & Fernandez, 1981).

22

BIOLOGICAL RESEARCH
ON TEMPERAMENT

We were convinced very quickly after we started our exploration of temperament in the NYLS that we could find no evidence showing a child's temperamental characteristics could be attributed to the parents' child care practices and attitudes. These attributes could only be inferred by us and a number of other temperament students to have some biological basis. This judgment could not, before the 1970s, be confirmed by hard research data, and one could only speculate then as to the nature of the biological factors that shaped temperament. But there are now substantial findings emerging from the sophisticated experiments of an increasing number of temperament researchers.

Twin studies of the comparison of same-sex, mono-, and dizogotic twin pairs have been a traditional strategy. Two infancy studies in the 1970s, one in this country (Buss & Plomin, 1975), the other in Norway (Torgersen & Kringlen, 1978), have reported evidence of a partial genetic basis for temperament.

Then, in 1984, Jerome Kagan and his coworkers at Harvard reported a distinguished study in which they found a correlation between heart rate and its variable and a cluster of temperamental characteristics called behavioral inhibition versus a group who were uninhibited (Kagan, Resnick, Clarke, Snidman, & Garcia-Coll, 1984). Kagan and colleagues defined this temperamental pattern as "uncertainty to the unfamiliar" (p. 2211). This definition is quite similar to our categorization of the temperamental cluster as slow-to-warm-up from the NYLS (Thomas et al., 1968).

Kagan and coworkers identified 43 four-year-old children of which 21 were classified as uninhibited and 22 as inhibited. The 43 children were observed, tested, and rated in two laboratory sessions with a number of simple task procedures. At the same time two electrodes were attached to each child in order to record heart rate. The ratings were analyzed quantitatively, and indication of marked behavioral inhibition versus uninhibition was statistically highly significant. The calculation of the comparison of heart rate and stability with the two groups of children showed that the inhibited children had higher and more stable heart rates than the uninhibited children.

This report by Kagan and his coworkers is detailed here because it was the first objective and sophisticated study with specific evidence of a biological correlation with temperament.

Kagan and his group have pursued this finding intensively at succeeding age periods, by comparing the correlations of other biological variables with behavioral inhibition. To summarize, at 5.5 years they have found significant correlations with heart rate and variability, pupillary dilation during cognitive stress, norepinephrine activity, cortisol level, and variability of the pitch periods of vocal utterances under cognitive stress. Kagan (1994) has emphasized that these correlations are not immutable, and environmental factors undoubtedly play a highly significant influence.

Kagan reviews briefly the findings of his group's studies in the most recent few years, and presents that "we believe, but cannot yet prove, that the excitability of the army of data and its circuits to the corpus striatum, locus striatum, hypothalamus central gray, and sympathetic nervous system participates in mediating the reactive and relaxed profiles we have described" (Kagan, 1994, p. 37).

FURTHER STUDIES

The succeeding years after Kagan et al.'s first report in 1984 were followed by an increasing number of research studies of neurochemical and neurophysiological correlations with various temperamental characteristics. To emphasize, "Recently, there has been an explosion of interest in the biological basis of behavior, and concepts of temperament are becoming rooted in concepts of complex biological processes" (Bates, Wachs, & Emde, 1994, p. 276).

This "explosion" was documented by the first temperament conference with a biological focus, held in October 1992 in Bloomington, Indiana. The published proceedings of the conference were edited by Bates and Wachs (1994), and citations from just a few of the chapters will illustrate the character of the reports: brain substrates of emotion and temperament; neural basis of infant temperament; and psychoendocrine studies of temperament and stress in early childhood.

These biological studies of temperament are an impressive beginning. The implications of the findings are clear. The debate of a biological versus an environmental basis can now be concluded. Temperament definitely has a biological source. Beyond this, the research emphasizes that temperament is not unidimensional. Environmental factors always influence biological issues, so that the constant interplay of biology and environment shapes the specific behavior of temperament from the earliest infancy to adult life.

23

TEMPERAMENT AND CULTURE

In the early 1970s, a young Dutch-American medical student, Martin deVries, became interested in the significance of culture in health and illness. He obtained a fellowship, with an approved deferment from his medical school, that supported him in pursuing a series of cultural studies in several tribes in Eastern Africa (deVries & deVries, 1977).

In his projects, deVries had been impressed by the importance of temperament reported in our publications. Among his areas of data collection and findings, he collected temperament data on children of the Masai tribe in Kenya. This was a primitive seminomadic tribe living in the sub-Sahara region. At a time when a severe drought was just beginning, DeVries obtained temperament ratings on 47 infants, age 2 to 4 months, using a translation of a standard questionnaire.

With these ratings, deVries identified the 10 infants with the most easy temperament and the 10 with the most difficult temperament using the temperament clusters of the NYLS study. He returned to this tribe 5 months later, by which time the drought had killed off 97% of the cattle. Despite the drought, DeVries was able to locate seven "easy" babies and six "difficult" ones. The families of the other infants had moved to unknown places in an attempt to escape the drought. Of the seven "easy" babies, five

185

had died, whereas all the "difficult"infants had survived (deVries, 1984).

How do we explain this most extraordinary event with the Masai children, when in industrialized societies, with few exceptions, most infants with easy temperament prosper, while those with difficult temperament do not?

There are two likely related explanations for the survival versus the death of those Masai infants. First the difficult infants cried long and loud; the easy infants whined. For their parents the intensive cries of the difficult infants might have indicated that they were the strong babies who would survive and so they were favored with the scarce food. Second these lusty cries might have indicated that these difficult children were likely to grow up to become strong warriors, an important virtue in this tribe, and hence favored them in food allocation. Unfortunately, those whimpering quietly with hunger might have been thought likely to die under this stress and also not to have the constitution of a future warrior.

This life and death situation faced by the Masai tribe dramatized the linkage of temperament and culture. The ecology of a seminomadic culture determined the survival of infants with a specific temperament. At the same time, the infants' temperamental behavior determined their parents' cultural judgments as to which infants were to be provided sufficient food.

DeVries also pursued the correlation in three East African societies. In this study, 178 infants differing on a number of environmental dimensions were examined to determine if aspects of their developmental environment influenced temperament characteristics. His data strongly suggested that cultural child rearing patterns, degree of modernization, maternal orientation, ecological setting, and specific early events contribute to temperament (deVries & Sameroff, 1984).

OTHER CULTURAL STUDIES

The relationship of culture and temperament has attracted the interest of a number of social psychologists and psychiatrists.

Dr. John McDermott, Jr., chairman of the department of psychiatry of the University of Hawaii, and his coworkers (1983) conducted cultural studies on the influence of family functioning on adolescent development, using a cross section from the community representing several major ethnic groups—Caucasian, Chinese, Japanese, and Hawaiian. Their extensive findings have been reported (McDermott et al., 1983), but here mention will be made only of the influence of temperament. McDermott and his coworkers summarized their research on culture and temperament: "From it, and our experience, we hypothesize that (1) the relationship between culture and temperament may constitute a dynamic fusion that changes with time (developmental stages) in a nonlinear, but not random way, and (2) "goodness of fit" varies with developmental stage and may have its own critical time periods. A new method of thinking may be needed to incorporate these complex, constantly interacting systems" (Gerhard, McDermott, & Andrade, 1994, p. 155). McDermott's hypotheses are plausible, and are indeed challenging for their implications for all of us.

Drs. Sara Harkness and Charles Super, husband and wife, both professors in the department of human development at Pennsylvania State University, have together pursued a number of research studies in anthropology and social psychology. Their special study was their comparative research in Kenya and the United States to define what temperamental characteristics are difficult for most families in the two settings, and also how families structure the pattern of familial responses to children with different dispositions. The researchers detailed the differences in the two very different cultures and the interactional processes with their specific temperamental characteristics, noting striking differences in the child's functioning (Super & Harkness, 1994). They concluded that "without a theory of temperament, psychological anthropology would have difficulty moving beyond the now abandoned notion of a prototypical personality shaped by each culture" (Super & Harkness, 1994, pp. 119–120).

Our own cross-cultural comparisons of the findings of the NYLS and the longitudinal study of Puerto Rican working class (PRWC) families have identified a number of differences in these two cultures. The protocols of gathering data on the children's behavior and the categorizations and temperamental ratings were identical for both samples. To avoid cultural bias, the interviews were conducted by women of Puerto Rican background, while the raters were identical for the NYLS and PRWC cohorts.

A comparison of the two samples showed marked differences in the temperament distributions only in rhythmicity and intensity. The comparison of the other seven categories showed no significant differences (Thomas & Chess, 1977, p. 147).

However, differences in a specific symptom from their temperament–culture interactional process was striking. Only one NYLS middle-class child out of 42 clinical cases presented excessive and uncontrollable motor activity, whereas eight of the 15 PRWC children did. Our judgment is that some, if not most, of the "hyperactivity" displayed by the latter group was due to the circumstances of their environment. The families lived in small apartments and the children were likely to be cooped up at home for fear of accidents in the street. For the temperamentally high activity children, this represented severe excessive stress. The children in the NYLS with similar temperament, by contrast, usually lived in spacious apartments or suburban homes, with adequate safe play space at home and in the neighborhood.

SUMMATION

The importance of the many factors found in the wide-spread studies of cross-cultural examination of different societies over the world has been documented. The reports cited in this chapter have clarified the indication that the information gathered regarding the temperamental characteristics of the individuals of a culture provides a useful additional tool to the analysis of cross-cultural programs. De Vries (1994), now a professor of social psychiatry at the University of Limburg, the Netherlands, amplifies McDermott's hypothesis with the statement that:

Individual differences take on varying significance depending on diverse factors in the environment, and that these influences shift over time even for the same individual. Competence or risk at any point in early development, whether reached through normal developmental processes or by the intervention of others, is not linearly related to the child's competence and performance at a later time. The cases make clear that in order to complete the equation of prediction one needs to add the effects of physical, social, cultural, and family environments. The environmental factors, however, yield their meaning only when they are brought into relationship with individual, constitutional characteristics such as infant temperament. Temperament brings maternal activities, the cultural plan, and environmental effects into perspective. Without this focus on the individual characteristics of the infant over time, or for that matter on the person in a larger medical frame of reference, understanding the environment and developmental transactions would be impossible. (de Vries, 1994, p. 138).

24

TEMPERAMENT IN CONSISTENCY AND CHANGE

As we originally began to observe the phenomenon of temperament clinically and impressionistically, we were struck by the many dramatic evidences of continuity in the individuals that we knew, sometimes from early childhood to adulthood. It was tempting to generalize from these instances to the concept that adults' temperamental characteristics could be predicted from a knowledge of their behavior style in early childhood. However, such a formulation would be completely at variance with our fundamental commitment to an interactionist viewpoint, in which individual behavioral development is conceived as a constantly evolving and changing process of organism—environment interaction.

All other psychological phenomena, such as intellectual competence, coping mechanisms, adaptive patterns, and value systems, can and do change over time. How could it be otherwise for temperament?

As we began systematically to follow the life course of the NYLS samples from infancy to early adult life, our doubts arose. We were convinced that there were a number of the subjects with change in temperament at various periods of their life course.

A dramatic instance is described in the case vignette of Carl presented in Chapter 15.

Carl belonged in the group with markedly difficult temperament in infancy, preschool age, and early school age. His functioning had changed to demonstrate easy temperament in middle childhood and adolescence, then changed back to difficult temperament in his first college year, and shifted once again to relatively easy temperament in his subsequent college years and following years of his personal and career life.

STUDIES OF CONSISTENCY

The search for consistency over time in temperament or any developmental variable has attracted researchers and theorists for a specific reason. Consistency can predict the course of behavioral development and indicate where and how to intercede to prevent behavior disorders in the future. Theories of development may take many forms: a hereditary and constitutional fixed basis, Freudian theory, Erikson's formulation, behaviorism, and sociological theories such as the culture of poverty. But most agree in asserting that later behavior derives directly and predictability from childhood patterns.

A number of quantitative studies of consistency in temperament over time have been done by researchers, including ourselves. McDevitt (1986) has reviewed these studies and concludes that they "do not permit firm conclusions to be made about the continuity of temperament." As to the qualitative reports, "what seems to emerge from these observations is the general notion that continuities in temperament are more enduring and more easily detected as the level of analysis becomes less specific . . . and more global or general" (pp. 35–36).

Beyond these limited quantitative findings, other critical researchers have listed a number of substantial methodological problems that interfere with the evidence of consistency over time. Rutter's (1970) cogent comments can be summarized: Of importance are the amount of development still to occur; modifiability by the child's subsequent experiences; effects of differing rates of maturation; and the changing context that the child's behavior might have on the behavioral ratings.

To summarize, the eminent developmental psychologist Robert McCall pointed out to temperament researchers that "the conceptual and statistical strategies typically used to study individual differences are designed to detect *lack* of change or development. It is an uninteresting and disappointing result." By contrast, McCall (1986) emphasized "that change is the essence of developmental disciplines and that we should be just as vigorous in describing change, whether in individual differences or developmental functions and whether in mental development or temperament, as we are in the search for stability and continuity" (p. 16).

THE CHALLENGE FOR THE STUDY OF CONSISTENCY AND CHANGE

We have documented significant change of temperament in some individual cases in our NYLS subjects and in the experience of other studies. But, basically, the reasons for change have been idiosyncratic in separate cases, and far removed from any systematic methodology.

The problem for change is similar with regard to consistency. The review by McDevitt has reported that the only systematic studies have found very modest sample correlations. Even if a presumably important finding of consistency will show a high correlation of .7, this only leaves the significance of 50%, and leaves the 50% variance unexplained.

But we cannot just ignore the issue of consistency. There are enough individual life span histories of clearcut, consistency; we are challenged to explain them. For

example, Karen's responses to new situations and new
people were typical of the slow-to-warm-up child in infancy and childhood. No problems developed because her
parents understood and accepted her behavioral patterns
and gave her enough time to adapt to new situations in
an unpressured way. One incident of interest occurred
when the nursery school had a special program for the
parents. When Karen came in with her mother and saw
the congregation of strange adults, she climbed onto her
mother's lap, stayed there all evening and refused to join
her group. As the mother described it, "All the other parents were looking at me, and I knew they were mentally
criticizing me for encouraging my daughter's clinging and
dependency." Fortunately for Karen, her mother was
amused by the experience, and not threatened by these
derogatory judgments of other parents.

Karen, when 16 years old, pursued this same developmental course. She had responded "warily" (as her
mother put it) to almost all new situations—a change of
school, a new summer group program, a new curriculum.
However, this initial slow-to-warm-up reaction had never
created avoidance or permanent withdrawal from stimulating situations and experiences. A new mathematics
course was difficult and distressful at first, but she per-
sisted and planned to take an elective course the next
year. Karen would ask her mother to call a new doctor or
dentist for the first appointment, but then took over all
the subsequent arrangements. She had many friends and
interests and became one of the student activity leaders.
She was assertive and appropriately independent for her
age, with no evidence of excessive dependency on her
parents or others.

Karen, with her temperament, had a smooth developmental course. She mastered the multitude of new situations over the years because her parents and teachers did
not place demands on her or pressure her at a pace that
would have been excessive for a slow-to-warm-up youngster. With these positive life experiences, now at 16 years,

Karen's academic and social activities are successful and clearly she has a high degree of self-esteem. Her successful functioning must have led her to know that she could cope smoothly with any new situations. Yet, in spite of all her experiences, she still responds to a new situation in the initial way; her uncomfortable first response shows her unchanged slow-to-warm-up temperamental pattern.

We are left with idiosyncratic case histories that are intriguing but do not shed light. We have yet to do a systematic study that will give us a depth of understanding of this phenomenon.

A PLAN FOR THE STUDY OF CONSISTENCY AND CHANGE

We have felt for years that the identification of the basic factors of consistency and/or change in temperament over time would provide significant information that would expand its usefulness for prevention, early intervention, and treatment in children, and perhaps even adults, with behavioral difficulties. But to our knowledge, no systematic investigation has been undertaken.

After pondering this challenge for many years, I (S.C.) have now developed a promising pilot study for an analytic method for such an investigation.

THE PILOT STUDY

From our NYLS data base I selected the complete data material of 30 subjects. The focus was on the ratings of intensity and the slow-to-warm-up cluster, each quite different behaviorally and each functionally important. The 15 highest and 15 lowest ratings at 3 years of these two temperamental categories were tabulated using our computer records. First, the intensity scores of each subject were listed in order by each age. At age 2 years, consistency or change from age 1 year was decided by comparison. Then I read thoroughly through all the data at 2 years and culled and listed all the items of the data that were pertinent to either consistency or change. With this same procedure from each sequential age (2 to 3, etc.) until adult life, consistency, or change of intensity was identified one age to the next.

After I had completed the list of the pertinent items that showed consistency or change in all the sequential years, using clinical judgment I grouped these items into six factors: social cognition, self-awareness of temperament, motivation, support network, self-esteem, and fortuitous events. Each of the factors was defined, and the appropriate specific items listed. A search of the similar factors found in the developmental literature served to refine the appropriate items.

Drs. Jacqueline and Richard Lerner, eminent developmental experts, reviewed my definitions, itemization, and ratings of my six factors and have refined them in detail. I proceeded with this same analysis of consistency and change of the slow-to-warm-up temperamental category.

NEXT METHODOLOGICAL TASKS

The Lerners, both professors of psychology at Michigan State University, had previously cooperated with us on a number of temperament projects. Both of them and we (S.C. and A.T.) agreed that the findings of the pilot study were promising enough to map out the next methodological steps of the project. Jacqueline and I (S.C.) took the major responsibility for the next tasks, and Richard and Alex (A.T.) served as consultants.

We formulated the sequential steps of the project:

1. Determine interratio reliabilities of the ratings of the six factors. (This is in progress.)

2. Once the interreliabilities are satisfactory, their ratings for each year of intensity and slow-to-warm-up will be scored.

3. With the rating scores of the six factors and the corresponding years of the temperament ratings, we could pose a number of complex quantitative analyses. For example, we could ask, "What weight for the influence of each factor for consistency and change of temperament both cross-sectional and longitudinal could be identified?" "What would be the correlations of each of the six factors and their significance?" These quantitative analyses require the ability of a highly expert statistician. Fortunately, one of the faculty of Michigan State, Dr. Alex Von Eye, who is recognized as an eminent statistical expert, had worked with the Lerners on several temperamental studies, and is available.

4. The quantitative findings of the project should shed light on the implications of the basic structure of temperament. Beyond this, the findings could be translated into a number of practical implications for the guidance of parents, teachers, and others for healthy child development and advice for the amelioration of troubled children.

CONCLUSION

This program for the study of consistency and change of temperament that we have mapped out is indeed a demanding and complex challenge. Clearly, we will require substantial financial support. If we do succeed in getting it, we will look ahead for the same model for the next program of the other temperamental categories. If our resources are insufficient, we are confident that our data of the pilot project and the beginnings of the entire ambitious project will be sufficient to report a number of suggestive and intriguing findings.

25

A LOOK TO THE FUTURE

The previous chapters have indicated that a number of current directions and activities promise significant explorations in the future: the dynamics of the continuity and change in temperament over time; the expansion of knowledge of the biological correlations of temperament, which will shed light on the intrinsic nature of temperament; and the use of temperament as a powerful tool in the study of the delineation of the cultural differences of ethnic, class, and social groups. The use of temperament as a factor in psychotherapy needs expansion and refinement regarding treatment not only of children and adolescents but also of adults; the role of temperament in the evaluation and treatment of a variety of psychological and clinical conditions requires clarification.

One important issue has not been discussed in this book or, in fact, in most American publications. Professor Jan Strelau and his colleagues in Poland have elaborated a comprehensive neo-Pavolvian system in their study of individual temperamental differences. Their work has transformed the traditional static and limited Russian Pavlovian studies by adding exploration of the correlation of Pavlovian concepts with basic widespread environmental factors. Both the Polish and Western European temperament researchers agree with the need for consideration of a biological–environmental dynamic for a fuller

understanding of the functional significance of temperament, but from different viewpoints. We have had a number of congenial discussions with Strelau and his colleagues, which have been interesting, but have so far not
led to joint collaborative programs that would be valuable
for both sides.

Finally, a basic challenge regarding the importance of a
commitment to temperament studies looking to the future
can be best posed by the statement of the distinguished
research and clinical developmental psychologist Judy
Dunn (1986):

> There are urgent practical questions toward which
> temperament research can be directed—child abuse,
> the response of children to stressful change, trau-
> matic experiences, or family discord. . . . On the
> other hand, some of the major issues in develop-
> mental psychology—the elucidation of the processes
> involved in developmental change, the different
> forms of individual–environment correlation, the ori-
> gins of differences in children's relationships with
> their family and friends—may well be illuminated by
> studies which include careful assessments of temper-
> amental differences in children. (p. 170).

REFERENCES

Alpert, A., Neubauer, P. W., & Wiel, A. P. (1956). Unusual
variation in drive endowment. In R. S. Eissler (Ed.),
Psychoanalytic study of the child (pp. 125–163). New
York: International Universities Press.

Bates, J. E., Wachs, T. D., & Emde, R. N. (1994). Toward
practical uses for biological concepts of temperament.
In J. E. Bates & T. D. Wachs (Eds.), *Temperament,
individual differences at the interface of biology and
behavior*. Washington, DC: American Psychological
Association.

Bergman, P., & Escalona, S. (1949). Unusual sensitivities in
very young children. In R.S. Eissler (Ed.),
Psychoanalytic study of the child (p. 33). New York:
International Universities Press.

Blos, P. (1979). *The adolescent passage*. New York: International Universities Press.

Brazelton, B. (1969). *Infants and mothers*. New York: Dell.

Brazelton, T. (1973). Neonatal behavioral assessment scale.
Clinics in Development Medicine, 50.

Bronson, W. C. (1974). Mother–toddler interaction: A
perspective on studying the development of competence.
Merrill-Palmer Quarterly, 20, 275–301.

Buss, A. H., & Plomin, R. (1975). *A temperamental theory of
personality development*. New York: Wiley.

Cameron, J. R., Hansen, R., & Rosen, D. (1989). Preventing behavioral problems in infancy through temperament assessment and parental support programs. In W. B. Carey & S. C. McDevitt (Eds.), *Prevention and early intervention* (pp. 157–167). New York: Brunner/Mazel.

Cameron, J. R., & Rice, D. C. (1986). Developing anticipatory guidance programs based on early assessment of infant temperament: Two tests of a prevention model. *Journal of Pediatric Psychology, 18,* 221–234.

Cameron, J. R., Rice, D., Hansen, R., & Rosen, D. (1994). Developing temperament guidance programs within pediatric practice. In W. B. Carey & S. C. McDevitt (Eds.), *Prevention and early intervention* (pp. 226–234). New York: Brunner/Mazel.

Cameron, J. R., Rice, D., Rosen, D. & Chesterman, E. (1996). Evaluating the clinical and cost effectiveness of a temperament-based anticipatory guidance program for parents of infants in a health maintenance organization. Manuscript submitted for publication.

Carey, W. B. (1970). A simplified method of determining infant temperament. *Journal of Pediatrics, 77,* 188–194.

Carey, W. B. (1986). Temperament and clinical practice. In S. Chess & A. Thomas (Eds.), *Temperament in clinical practice* (p. 239). New York: Guilford.

Carey, W. B., & McDevitt, S. C. (1989). *Clinical and educational applications of temperament research.* Berwyn, PA: Swets North America.

Carey, W. B., & McDevitt, S. C. (1995). *Coping with children's temperament.* New York: Basic Books.

Chess, S. (1979). Academic lecture. Developmental theory revisited: Findings of a longitudinal study. *Canadian Journal of Psychiatry, 24,* 101–112.

Chess, S., & Fernandez, P. (1981). *The handicapped children school.* New York: Brunner/Mazel.

Chess, S., Korn, S. J., & Fernandez, P. B. (1971). *Psychiatric disorders of children with congenital rubella.* New York: Brunner/Mazel.

Chess, S. & Thomas, A. (1984). *Origins and evolution of behavior disorders.* New York: Brunner/Mazel.

Chess, S., & Thomas, A. (1986). Temperament in clinical practice. New York: Guilford Press.

Clarke, A. M., & Clarke, A. M. B. (1976). *Early experience: Myth and evidence.* London: Open Books.

Coleman, J. C. (1978). Current contradictions in adolescent theory. *Journal of Youth and Adolescence, 7,* 1–11.

Costello, A. (1975). Are mothers stimulating? In R. Lewis (Ed.), *Child alive* (pp. 45–46). London: Temple Smith.

deVries, M. W. (1984). Temperament and infant mortality among the Masai of East Africa. *American Journal of Psychiatry, 141,* 1189–1194.

deVries, M. (1994). Kids in context: Temperament in cross-cultural perspective. In W. B. Carey and S. C. McDevitt (Eds.), *Prevention and early intervention,* New York: Brunner/Mazel.

deVries, M. W., & deVries, M. R. (1977). Cultural relativity of toilet training readiness. *Pediatrics, 60,* 170–179.

deVries, M. W., & Sameroff, A. J. (1984). Culture and temperament: Influences on infant temperament in three East African Societies. *American Journal of Orthopsychiatry, 54,* 83–96.

Dubos, R. (1965). *Man adapting.* New Haven: Yale University Press.

Dunn, J. (1986). Commentary: Issues for future research. In R. Plomin & J. Dunn (Eds.), *The study of temperament: Changes, continuities and challenges* (pp. 163–171). Hillsdale, NJ: Erlbaum.

Dunn, J., & Kendrick, C. (1980). Studying and temperament and parent–child interactions: Comparison of interview and direct observation. *Developmental Medicine and Child Neurology, 22,* 484–496.

Eisenberg, L. (1994). Advocacy for the health of the public. In W. B. Carey & S. C. McDevitt (Eds.), *Prevention and early intervention* (p. 285). New York: Brunner/Mazel.

Eissler, K. R. (1958). Notes on problems of techniques in the psychoanalytic treatment of adolescents. *Psychoanalytic Study of the Child, 13,* 233–254.

Erikson, E. H. (1959). Identity and the life cycle. *Psychological Issue, 1,* 116.

Fishman, M. E. (1982). *Child and youth activities of the National Institute of Mental Health 1981–1982.* Washington: Alcohol, Drug Abuse and Mental Health Administration.

Freud, A. (1958). Adolescence. *Psychoanalytic Study of the Child, 13*, 255–278.

Freud, A. (1960). The child guidance as a center of prophylaxis and enlightenment. In J. Weinreb (Ed.), *Recent developments in psychoanalytic child therapy* (pp. 25–38). New York: International Universities Press.

Freud, S. (1950). Analysis, terminable and interminable. In J. Strachey (Ed. and Trans.), *Collected works* (Vol. 5, p. 316). London: Hogarth. (Original work published 1937)

Fries, M., & Woolf, P. (1953). Some hypotheses on the role of the congenital activity type of personality development. In R. S. Eissler (Ed.), *Psychoanalytic study of the child* (pp. 48–62). New York: International Universities Press.

Gerhard, A. L., McDermott, J. F., Jr., & Andrade, N. N. (1994). Variations in cultural influences in Hawaii. In W. B. Carey & S. C. McDevitt (Eds.), *Prevention and early intervention*. New York: Brunner/Mazel.

Gesell, A., & Ames, L. B. (1937). Early evidences of individuality in the human infant. *Journal of Genetic Psychology, 47*, 339.

Hall, G. S. (1904). *Adolescence* (Vol. 11, p. 74). New York: Appleton.

Hunt, J. V. (1980). Implications of plasticity and hierarchical achievements for the assessment of development and risk of mental retardation. In D. D. Savin, R. C. Hawkins, L. V. Walker, & J. H. Penticuss (Eds.), *Exceptional infant*. New York: Brunner/Mazel.

Kagan, J. (1971). *Change and continuity in infancy*. New York: Wiley.

Kagan, J. (1994). Inhibited and uninhibited temperaments. In W. B. Carey & S. C. McDevitt (Eds.), *Prevention and early intervention*. New York: Brunner/Mazel.

Kagan, J., & Moss, H. A. (1962). *Birth to maturity*. New York: Wiley.

Kagan, J., Resnick, J. S., Clarke, C., Snidman, N., & Garcia-Coll (1984). Behavioral inhibition to the unfamiliar. *Child Development, 55*, 2212–2225.

Keogh, B. K. (1982). Children's temperament and teacher decisions. In R. Porter & G. Collins (Eds.), *Ciba*

Foundation Symposium 89: Temperamental differences in infants and young children (pp. 267–278). London: Pitman.

Keogh, B. K. (1989). Temperament research and school. In G. A. Kohnstamn, J. E. Bates, & M. J. Rothbart (Eds.), *Temperament in childhood* (pp. 436–450). New York: Wiley.

Korner, A. (1973). Sex differences in newborns with special reference to differences in the organization of oral behavior. *Journal of Child Psychology and Psychiatry, 14*, 19–29.

Kurcinka, M. (1991). *Raising your spirited child*. New York: HarperCollins.

Lerner, R. M., Palermo, M., Spiro, A., & Nesselrode, J. R. (1982). Assessing the dimensions of temperamental individuality across the life span: The dimensions of temperament survey (DOTS). *Child Development, 53*, 149–159.

Levine, M. D., Carey, W. B., & Crocker, A. C. (1992). *Developmental–behavioral pediatrics* (2nd ed.). Philadelphia: W. B. Saunders.

Levy, D. (1943). *Maternal overprotection*. New York: Columbia University Press.

Martin, R. P. (1982). Activity level, distractibility and persistence: Critical characteristics in early schooling. In G. A. Kohnstamn, J. E. Bates, & M. J. Rothbart (Eds.), *Temperament in childhood* (pp. 451–461). New York: Wiley.

McCall, R. B. (1986). Issues of stability and continuity in temperament research. In R. Plomin & J. Dunn (Eds.), *The study of temperament: Changes, continuities and challenges* (p. 16). Hillsdale, NJ: Erlbaum.

McClowry, S. G., Giangrande, S. K., Tommasini, N. R., Clinton, W., Foreman, N. S., Lynch, K., & Ferketich, S. (1994). The effects of child temperament, maternal characteristics, and family circumstances on the maladjustment of school-age children. *Research in Nursing and Health, 17*, 25–35.

McDermott, J. F., Robillard, A. B., Cher, W. F, Hsu, J., Tseng, W. S., & Ashton, G. C. (1983). Reexamining the concept of adolescence: Differences between adolescent boys and girls in the context of their families. *American Journal of Psychiatry, 140*, 1318–1322.

McDermott, J. M., Jr. (1994). Variations in cultural diversity. In W. B. Carey & S. C. McDevitt (Eds.), *Prevention and early intervention.* (pp. 149–160). New York: Brunner/ Mazel.

McDevitt, S. C. (1986). Continuity and discontinuity of temperament in infancy and early childhood: A psychometric perspective. In R. Plomin & J. Dunn (Eds.), *The study of temperament: Changes, continuities and challenges* (pp. 35–36). Hillsdale NJ: Erlbaum.

McFarlane, J. W., Allen, W., & Honzig, M. P. (1962). *A development study of the behavior problems of normal children between 24 months and 14 years.* Berkeley: University of California.

Meili, R. (1959). A longitudinal study of personality development. In L. Jessner & E. Pavenstedt (Eds.), *Dynamic psychopathology in childhood* (pp. 106–123). New York: Grune & Stratton.

Melvin, N. (1995). Children's temperament: Intervention for parents. *Journal of Pediatric Nursing, 10*, 152–159.

Melvin, N., & McClowry, S. G. (1995). Editorial. *Journal of Pediatric Nursing, 10*, 140.

Murphy, L. B. (1962). *The widening world of childhood.* New York: Basic Books.

Offer, O., & Offer, J. (1975). *From teenage to young manhood.* New York: Basic Books.

Pavlov, I. P. (1927). *Conditioned reflexes: An investigation of the physiological activity of the cerebral cortex.* London: Oxford University Press.

Pullis, M., & Cadwell, J. (1982). The influence of children's temperament characteristics on teacher's decision strategies. *American Education Research Journal, 19*, 165–181.

Rutter, M. (1970). Psychological development: Predictions from infancy. *Journal of Child Psychiatry and Psychology, 11*, 49–62.

Rutter, M. (1979). *Changing youth in a changing society.* London: Nuffield Provincial Hospitals Trust.

Shirley, M. M. (1933). *The first two years: A study of twenty-five babies.* Minneapolis: University of Minnesota Press.

Smith, B. (1994). The temperament program: Community based prevention of behavior disorders in children. In W. B. Carey & S. C. McDevitt (Eds.), *Prevention and early intervention* (pp. 257–266). New York: Brunner/Mazel.

Super, C. M., & Harkness, S. (1994). Temperament and the developmental niche. In W. B. Carey & S. C. McDevitt (Eds.), *Prevention and early intervention* (pp. 115–125). New York: Brunner/Mazel.

Thomas, A., & Chess, S. (1977). *Temperament and development.* New York: Brunner/Mazel.

Thomas, A., Chess, S., & Birch, H. G. (1968). *Temperament and behavior disorders in childhood* (pp. 137–138). New York: Brunner/Mazel.

Thomas, A., Mittelman, M., Chess, S., Korn, S. J., & Cohen, J. (1982). A temperament questionnaire for early adult life. *Educational and Psychological Measurement, 42,* 593–600.

Torgersen, A., & Kringlen, E. (1978). Genetic aspects of temperamental differences in infants. *Journal of American Academy of Child Psychiatry, 17,* 433–444.

Turecki, S. (1989). The difficult child center. In W. B. Carey & S. C. McDevitt (Eds.), *Prevention and early intervention.* (pp. 141–153). New York: Brunner/Mazel.

Turecki, S., with Torner, L. (1989, rev.). *The difficult child* (pp. 3–5). New York: Bantam.

Weissbluth, M. (1987). *Sleep well.* London: Unwin Paperbacks.

Weisz, J. R., & Sigman, M. (1993). Parent reports of behavioral and emotional problems among children in Kenya, Thailand, and the United States. *Child Development, 64,* 98–109.

Wenar, C. (1963). The reliabilities of developmental histories. *Psychosomatic Medicine, 25,* 505.

Whaley, L. F., & Wong, D. L. (1983). *Nursing care of infants and children.* St. Louis, MO: C.V. Mosby.

Wilson, R. S., & Matheny, A. P., Jr. (1983). Assessment of infant twins. *Developmental Psychology, 19,* 172–183.

NAME INDEX

SUBJECT INDEX